Praise for My Husband's Under Here Somewhere

"A wonderful, slightly terrifying book! Combining fabulous and disturbing stories, as well as detailed science, *My Husband's Under Here Somewhere* is a great read for everyone, including those among us with the impulse to hold on to things, along with the folks who must live with them, and families torn apart by piles of ratty old newspapers and twine. This book is very helpful to me as a counselor and as a human with a distinct propensity for clutter."
—Deborah Allen, M.A., counselor and chronic pain educator.

"The personalized stories are quite compelling and clearly document the serious challenges of hoarding. It is a distinct privilege to read this engrossingly comprehensive review of people with this problem, as well as those with compulsive behaviors and hoarding found in other forms of mental illness."
—John Gillette, M.D., psychiatrist, Santa Cruz County Mental Health.

"This book presents broad based clinical details, alongside poignant pictures of the individual who is trapped among his or her belongings. Offering unique insights into a disorder that is both peculiar in its symptomatology and heartbreaking in its capacity to disable, it goes a long way toward dispelling the stereotype that hoarding is simply an irrational response to being a "child of the Depression.""
—Paul Bellina, MFT, mental health acute services.

"At times humorous, sometimes shocking but also enlightening at every turn, this is a fascinating read!"
—Ellen Morse-Weston, P.H.N., B.S.N., R.N.

"The history, along with degrees of hoarding, are clearly presented in a most readable fashion. The spiritual and societal aspects of materialism are also discussed with superb insight and nuance. *My Husband's Under Here Somewhere* should be on everyone's bookshelf, as long as you don't hoard it all to yourself. To be gleeful about such a serious matter may sound cold, but it is with great joy that I recommend this excellent, if not brilliant work.
—Gabriel Constans, Ph. D., grief and trauma therapist, educator, author.

My Husband's Under Here Somewhere

Works by William Strubbe:

Fiction:
Lullaby for Yossi: A Reincarnational Love Story
The Black Diaries: The Life of an Irish Rebel and Unrepentant Pervert
The Black Witch Moth and the Moonflower
Close Encounters of the Queer Kind: Collection of Short Stories and Poems

Non-Fiction:
The Reluctant Convert:
The Intersecting Spiritual Journeys of a Missionary,
a Housewife, her Gay Son and Bunch of Cats
Feathered Spirits: Winged Visitations from the Other Side

Plays:
The Wardrobe
Baby, Cradle and All
Family....In the Third Degree
The Healing Wall

Works by Janice Strubbe Wittenberg:

Fiction:
The Worship of Walker Judson

Non-Fiction:
The Rebellious Body: Reclaim Your Life from
Environmental Illness or Chronic Fatigue Syndrome

My Husband's Under Here Somewhere:

Collectors, Packrats, and Compulsive Hoarders

William C. Strubbe
Janice Strubbe Wittenberg, R.N.

Spiral Publishing
Aptos, California, U.S.A.
2017

Spiral Publishing
P.O. Box 2054, Aptos, CA, 95001-2054

Copyright 2017 William C. Strubbe and Janice Strubbe Wittenberg R.N.
All rights reserved.
No part of this book may be reproduced, scanned or distributed in any printed or electronic form without permission.
Please purchase only authorized editions.

Published in the United States by Spiral Publishing
Strubbe-Wittenberg.com

Library of Congress Cataloging-in-Publications Data
Strubbe, William; Strubbe Wittenberg, Janice
My Husband's Under Here Somewhere: Collectors, Packrats, and Compulsive Hoarders:
non-fiction/
William Strubbe, Janice Strubbe Wittenberg

ISBN-13: 9780989562324
ISBN-10: 0989562328

Library of Congress Control Number: 2017903544
Printed in the United States of America on acid-free paper

First edition

Cover design by: William Strubbe & Janice Strubbe Wittenberg
Interior art by: Bonni Carver
Editor: Hugh Cook
Authors' photograph: Ruel Walker

My Husband's Under Here Somewhere: Collectors, Packrats, and Compulsive Hoarders is based on facts. However, the names of many individuals as well as actual events have been altered and composited to protect confidentiality.

This Book is Dedicated to:

The Peace Pilgrim
A woman calling herself "Peace Pilgrim" eschewed all possessions except the clothes on her body and between 1953 to 1981, walked more than 25,000 miles on a personal pilgrimage.
Vowed to "remain a wanderer until mankind has learned the way of peace," she led a simple, joy-filled life.
Her profound message touched the hearts, minds, and lives of thousands.

And to Janice's beloved pal, Joyce Johnson Robinson: trusted work partner and sometime side-kick.
Many a life has vastly improved as a result of her amazingly kind ministrations.

Table of Contents

Introduction: What a Dump!—To Have and to
Hold Ever More · xiii

Chapter 1 This Hoarder's So-Called Life—One That's Gone to
the Dogs · 1
Chapter 2 Clutter Busters Strike Again—The Business of Cleanup · · · · · 14
Chapter 3 Animals do it, Humans do it—A Brief History of
Hoarding· ·21
Chapter 4 Collector, Packrat, or Hoarder?—It's a Fine Line· · · · · · · · · · ·31
Chapter 5 I'm Collecting as Fast as I can—OCD, with OCD
Hoarding as a Sub-Set· 44
Chapter 6 Hoarding Cats and Dogs—Loving Animals to Death· · · · · · ·62
Chapter 7 Evolution Gone Gonzo—Contributing Factors
and Hoarding Research· 77
Chapter 8 Look, Ma, No More Stuff!—Therapeutic Treatments for
Hoarders ·91
Chapter 9 Light at Dumpster's Bottom—Communities and
Neighbors Interface with Hoarders · · · · · · · · · · · · · · · · · · 114
Chapter 10 Till Trash do Us Part— Living with or Without
Your Beloved Hoarder ·136
Chapter 11 Scraping Out the Dead—Hoarders Who Die
Amidst Their Stuff ·149
Chapter 12 Got Affluenza?—The Spiritual Ramifications of
Our Junk· ·158

Endnotes: Sources—The Who, What, Where and the When, but
Not the Why or the How· ·177
About the Authors ·189

INTRODUCTION

What a Dump!—To Have and to Hold Ever More

"Trying to be happy by accumulating possessions is like trying to satisfy hunger by taping sandwiches all over your body."

—GEORGE CARLIN.

THE RED T-SHIRT I USUALLY wore on the job read, "Obey Me." And one time, I facetiously returned to a recalcitrant client's home flailing a cat-o-nine-tails. Yet, those whips and paddles in my arsenal were more figurative than literal, as I already held the upper hand.

A potential client dialing up Clutter Busters had already traversed the critical boundary to acknowledge their helplessness in the face of amassed clutter to seek my authoritative cattle-prod. Willing to pay a professional organizer to help deconstruct their chaos, they actually tolerated my bossiness.

Given the operative words, *Obey Me*, my clients usually did. Although I joked around and tried to make the process fun, I could be unflinchingly strict when necessary.

Whereas mild collectors simply needed my assistance to clean out their garage, or to arrange a home office, or to sort through possessions after the death of a spouse, others were truly desperate. One gentleman shoved a dresser in front of a bursting closet to keep it shut; another rented parking space because he'd crammed his garage so full of newspapers and garbage that no car, nor even another twig, could fit; another's husband gave her an ultimatum—her stuff or him.

Tellingly, she chose her stuff!

Early on in my clutter-busting career, it dawned on me that these worst-cases weren't just lazy bums, but that something beyond run-of-the-mill human behavior was at play. As a result, I should have been forewarned when one prospective client asked by phone if I had a pickup truck. Later, when the door opened to his San Francisco flat, as if something dead lay waiting, the stench bowled me over.

Quickly recovered, I managed to summon my best Bette Davis voice to remark, "What a dump!"—It literally was!

Until one experiences a house like this, it's easy to deem my account more fiction than fact. Yet his five-room Victorian was only accessible via narrow trails that blazed through waist-high accumulations of garbage. The bed had disappeared beneath drifts of clothes and books, as well as newspapers. Various other unimaginable items further filled the room. In the kitchen, dishes, pots, and pans, encrusted with blackened crud were jammed in the sink. Food and suspiciously scary items also spilled onto all countertops, and covered the floor, as well.

As a furry creature scampered, then disappeared beneath a pile of rubble, I squeaked and shuddered. And the bathroom: well, I'll skip the details…

Turned to my prospective client, who perched atop a couch arm that jutted out from the junk, I blurted, "Really...just a pickup truck? I need a dump truck and bulldozer to excavate this!"

To this the man blithely inquired, "Can you do it by Friday? My landlord's going to evict me unless it's all taken away."

When asked how he planned to pay me, he replied with a majestic arm sweep, "I figured there'd be things you'd want in trade."

Thinking I might've overlooked some fabulous treasure, I scanned the room. Then it hit: This fellow wasn't your run-of-the-mill slob with an aversion to the garbage pail. To his mind, ALL his stuff held value!

Annoyance waning, I wished him good luck, and departed. With stench still lingering in my clothes and hair; I couldn't wait to get home to shower.

Who doesn't know someone, be it a kooky cousin, a dear friend, a reclusive neighbor, or, heaven forbid, a beloved spouse, who dwells in a purgatory of clutter, thereby risking eviction, as well as ostracism, to say nothing of having to face legal battles, all for the sake of their junk. These unfortunate souls, beset with the irresistible urge to fill their homes, garages, yards, and storage-after-storage space with infinite amounts of seemingly useless gewgaws are locked in an immense struggle.

While the public-at-large may deem them lazy, wacko, confused, or terminally indecisive, the extreme hoarder is in the throes of a very real illness and cannot help him or herself. These people are unable to throw anything away, even if their well-being and life depend on it. In extreme cases, as John Gillette, M.D., staff psychiatrist with Santa Cruz County Mental Health can attest, it may boil down to precisely this: "Obsessive-compulsive hoarding is a confounding disorder that's difficult to treat, and in severe cases, can be life-threatening."

Scavenger, clutterer, packrat, and *junkaholic* are kindred longstanding terms for the word, *hoarder,* but the clinical appellation, *obsessive-compulsive hoarder* fills a relatively new niche in psychiatric circles. With the 2013 release of the DSM-5—the *Diagnostic and Statistical Manual of Mental Disorders*, which is the venerated diagnostic standard used by mental health professionals—hoarding was newly classified as a disorder unto itself. Yet hoarding as a mental health disorder remains little understood and also has the dubious distinction of being the most challenging of the obsessive-compulsive spectrum disorders to treat.

⌂⌂ ⌂

Several studies conducted by hoarding expert Randy Frost, Ph. D., along with another research project performed by the National Institute of Mental Health, estimate that between 2% and 3% of the U.S. population suffers from an obsessive-compulsive disorder (OCD) of some sort. Although other types of hoarding exist, most appear to be a subset of OCD, with about 15% to 30% of OCD sufferers—roughly 2 million Americans—who experience hoarding as their primary, most debilitating symptom. As awareness regarding the nature and complexity of this problem grows, these numbers will likely increase.[1,2]

Hoarders can be divided into two subgroups: *generalists* and *specialists*. *Generalists* collect any object known to humankind. They tend to acquire household items, clothes, trash, or freebies, along with readily available materials, including newspapers, junk mail, receipts, and magazines.

My first encounter with a hoarder was a *generalist* who also collected animals. Jean, a friend of my mother's, was intelligent, well-educated, and elegantly attractive. Despite many positives, however, love seemed to elude her. Eventually, I grasped why this was. Should a prospective suitor set foot in her home, he no doubt got an eyeful and never returned.

Given the clutter underfoot inside, it was tricky to walk about and her stairs were particularly hazardous to climb. Her bed, covered with clothes, papers, dishes, books, and memorabilia afforded little space to recline, so she slept upright in a chair alongside.

Status as an unrepentant hoarder notwithstanding, her life's mission, although admirable, involved the rescue of stray and unwanted animals. Any given week, five or six crated dogs barked in the kitchen, and dozens of cats swept through the house as if a feline tide.

Her living room's most impressive feature, comprised myriad careening stacks of newspapers and magazines that covered all floors, tables, couches, and chairs. Summoning nerve, I once asked why she kept it all.

"Someday," she replied, "I plan to clip articles of interest." It bears note that hoarders always intend at some future date to attend to their treasures. Yet that day never arrives. "Also," she added, "I stack papers on furniture to keep the cats from urinating on the upholstery."

As I eyed a particularly hideous, yet unobstructed armchair, she further elucidated, "I keep that one free so my cats have place to urinate."

Thankfully, we soon retired to the porch for fresh air and refreshments.

The *specialist* accumulates a specific category of items. Such items may include mountains of books and printed materials; or boxes electronic devices; or may involve collecting a particular type of animal. *Manx* cats, rare birds, rabbits or horses, for example, appeal to some. Vintage autos give others a thrill. There are those with a penchant for clothes from another era. One hoarder's treasure consisted of nearly a half a century's accumulation of soap remnants. Another odd one: Daniel's passion was lint.

How Daniel's attention riveted to lint, and what the appeal, eludes. With strands of thread and fluff-balls peeking out from beneath his sofa and mattress, and other threads and filaments spilling from drawers and cupboards, he constantly twined fluffy balls together.

Needless-to-say, he adored laundromats!

Then there's Norman. Gums denuded of teeth, this guy was the sweetest man ever. Back when McDonald's offered colorful boxes for their Happy Meal burgers, his affinity was so intense that he filled his entire home with them. When unable to get her husband to remove the debris, Norman's wife of twenty-six years gave him the boot.

Billionaire playboy Howard Hughes saved his fingernail and toenail clippings. Some treasure hair or skin flakes, as well. One elderly woman and her grown son, used a spare bedroom as their lavatory, accumulated years of fecal material. A former suffragette and poet aggregated her urine in murky gallon bottles; another kept shorn hair in Tupperware containers; another fellow shat in his socks, then tidily returned them to dresser drawers.

As the hoarder ages, he or she faces an escalating series of stressors—loss of control over bodily functions, the onslaught of illness, poor or limited finances, estrangement from loved ones, social isolation, retirement or being fired from one or many jobs, the death of a spouse, as well as the diminished ability to care for oneself. When such downturns occur, hoarding tends to escalate. A possible reason for this: hoarding activities help create an imaginary line of defense against loss.

Rather than relinquish independence and surrender to the organizing services provided by retirement communities or convalescent facilities, increased numbers of Baby Boomers opt to remain in their homes. This decision to "age in place" prompts experts to predict a marked increase in the prevalence of hoarding—in particular, dementia-related hoarding.

"The average age for those with hoarding problems is about fifty, yet many are older," notes Gail Steketee, Professor at Boston University. "There's a growing concern on the part of elder service workers about hoarding and how to manage its potential consequences, including fire and health hazards, risk of falling, and the inability to find medications."

Thankfully, public awareness regarding hoarding, as it relates to obsessive-compulsive disorders, is on the rise. Given the millions who avidly followed television shows such as *Hoarders*, *Hoarding: Buried Alive*, and Animal Planet's series *Confessions: Animal Hoarding*, hoarding is now a topic of fascination. While many watch such programs to be entertained or to be grossed out, few are able to fathom how difficult it is to live like that.

An attempted glimpse is offered by Sally Fields, who stars in the film, *Hello, My Name is Doris*, about an emotionally stunted older woman with a tendency to hoard. Years ahead of its time, there was also the televised series

Monk. The detective in the show is beset with tics and compulsions—which are OCD behaviors—and his agoraphobic brother, played by John Turturro, hoards junk.

Indeed, hoarding is often a family affair!

As I embarked on my odyssey to try to understand this phenomenon, as well as the folks impacted by it, I enlisted the expertise of my sister, Janice Strubbe Wittenberg. With over thirty-five years spent as a mental health nurse, seventeen of them as Santa Cruz County's sole crisis outreach worker, she's encountered many a hoarder.

Initially, I chalked up her fascinatingly peculiar tales about these people as mere embellishment, but later had to apologize for doubting her. Many of her experiences working with hoarders are conveyed on these pages.

All incidents described in this book are based on the authors' experiences, but in the interest of clarity, William's contributions are written in the first person, while Janice is identified by name when she gives input. It bears further mention, that my sister and I were equal partners in this project. She supplied all clinical information with regard to research and treatment, along with the historical and current day tales.

One individual who suffers from this disorder urged, "Please go ahead, it's important to tell our stories."

Yet, it's a delicate balance to decide what can and cannot be said. To protect privacy—with the exception of certain professionals, and the mention of stories relayed by the news media at large—all names of clients, as well as their families are changed. Additionally, each case described, including identifying details, has been altered, fictionalized, and composited to further render those involved unrecognizable.

Use of humor can be touchy when applied to an issue as serious as hoarding, yet we hope its application will enable the reader to absorb such difficult material with greater ease and that no offense will be taken. While these pages may help increase understanding as to this nightmarish problem, it's not a self-help book, and shouldn't pose as a substitute for seeking professional help

We *do* intend this work of lively observation and musing to prompt contemplation of one's own acquisitiveness and excess. In this process, it may become clear to the reader that they share traits in common with hoarders.

CHAPTER 1

This Hoarder's So-Called Life— One That's Gone to the Dogs

"In this world there are only two tragedies. One is not getting what one wants and the other is getting it."

—Oscar Wilde's Lament

MY HOARDING ARTICLE, APPEARING IN *Common Ground* magazine, spurred Patty to give me a call. In a twitter as we spoke, she explained that she taught journalism and English, then became an executive secretary for a high-tech firm, and later supplemented her income as a psychic reader. During those happier times, she enjoyed brisk walks along the trails near her home and swam regularly at the public pool. Our conversation culminated when she insisted that I pay a visit to hear more of her story.

Intelligent and well-spoken by phone, with wide-ranging interests that include singing and juggling; I found myself hard-pressed to envision her as anything but normal.

Until I pulled up in front of her double-wide mobile home, that is.

Assorted objects jutting from beneath their folds, an ocean of blue tarps swaddle much of the property. Those tarps cover piles of boxes and also hold newspapers in check to prevent them from blowing about. As if a yard sale is in progress, all space not covered by tarpaulins is strewn with junk. An eclectic array of stuff spills onto the door stoop and covers a side patio. The car, parked beneath the carport, is also jammed to the hilt.

On approach, as I spot a tidal wave of unidentified objects pressed and piled up against the front window, I brace myself.

"Howdy there, and welcome to my fantastic kingdom!" Patty calls out cheerily.

Garbed in a hibiscus-splashed mu-mu, Patty's brown wig is slightly askew. Resisting an urge to adjust it, I exclaim, "You're right, it's—er, quite a sight!"

"I'm such an extreme hoarder, I fear I'll never control my life," 62-year-old Patty confesses as we enter her abode. "I receive behavioral therapy and also take medication to stop the hoarding. Frankly, though, I'm not sure I'm ready to give it up. 'Cause, really, hoarding is my entire life."

Patty grew up in Oklahoma among an idyll of acreage comprised of lawns, vegetable gardens, and orchards, where she enjoyed pets and livestock and loved to loll about in the barn's hayloft. Although poor, her family rarely lacked the necessities, as they harvested fruit and vegetables, canning the land's bounty to fill pantry and cellar.

Thanks to her resourceful dad, the family weathered the Great Depression without succumbing to the soup line. Despite a mere third-grade education, Patty's father worked thirty years as a heavy equipment operator for the gas company. Additionally, he fished, hunted, and was a consummate scavenger.

"Daddy used to answer the phone so cheerily," Patty recalls, "saying *'Johnson's Junkyard.'* Even after surgery to fuse his spine, he frequented the dump to scavenge and haul home trailer-loads of junk, which he then used to build and repair buildings on our property."

Patty lauds her eight-room playhouse, situated beneath a stand of elms, as her favorite place. Her dad cobbled it together by fastening together wire cages, then affixed them with scrap board. She then furnished it with assorted reclaimed treasures. Dinged loving cups got used as dishes, and she used crates, vinyl car seats, and car hoods for furniture.

Like father like daughter, Patty's acquisitive nature seeded at an early age. Previously, I'd learned this was common, as the tendency to hoard can be passed from generation to generation.

Typically, hoarding begins early in life; it's even noted in three-year-olds. For young ones, however, parents control what their children possess and how cluttered their environment is allowed to become, so the depth of the issue may go undetected for a time.

What may be evident early on is the intense attachment youngsters develop to various objects and their tendency to apply human characteristics to them. In junior high, Patty ardently clipped thousands of articles on grooming and etiquette, then pasted them into scrapbooks. Too busy to bother absorbing the articles' contents, she preferred to busily collect and assemble still more of them.

Hoarding becomes a moderate challenge in one's twenties and thirties, and tends to bloom, full-tilt, as the individual approaches his or her forties and fifties. For some reason hoarding begins at a younger age for women than for men, but more males hoard than females. Should it begin at late onset, hoarding is often coupled with loss of some kind: divorce, death, declining health, or reduced independence. Stress and trauma are commonly noted in the early lives of hoarders and the compulsion to collect tends to flare during rough stretches.

Patty's mother, I gather, was coldly remote, and had a terrible temper. "My mom was such a grump," Patty recounts. "She habitually tossed out a lot of the stuff Daddy and I so carefully collected. So basically, he and I avoided her."

⌂⌂ ⌂

There are two types of hoarders: *primary* and *secondary,* and Patty fits the category of primary hoarder. *Primary* hoarding is generally characterized by those with intense feelings for the objects they collect. As a result, these folks are overly enamored with their junk and undergo extreme distress at the mere notion of its removal. And further, they're extraordinarily resistant to cleanup and intervention.

Secondary hoarders live in clutter and squalor as a result of a psychological or neurological malady, or possibly due to dementia, and aren't particularly attached to their stuff. Beset with an additional constellation of challenges, some fail to get rid of garbage as a result of mental or physical decline. Unable to organize their surroundings, these individuals usually don't grieve when hoarded objects are purged.

Back to Patty; books are her fondest treasures. "Open the cover," she declares, "and schwing...I go into a trance. As a girl, I envisioned the day when my own home would have wall-to-wall bookshelves that overflowed with books!"

Unfortunately, dreams do come true; for there I stood, mouth agape, eyeing Patty's bookshelf-lined walls. With a book collection that rivaled the stock found in many a bookstore, the jam-packed shelves were so numerous that no daylight could enter via windows, and her precariously stacked tomes consumed all floor space.

"My guess, I possess some 60,000 volumes," she announces, caressing several book covers. "Favorite topics include psychology, religion, art, history, magic, conjuring, psychic phenomena, antiques, collectibles, biography, martial arts, and I can't get enough detail about the lives of films stars."

Despite a buried stove top, she's managed to keep the sink available. "It's dandy that I don't have to use the bathroom to wash dishes or to get water.

Recently, I located the microwave and cleared out its innards so I can heat soup and chili. Here—" she thrusts a scaly, noodle-filled bowl at me, "—want some?"

Stomach roiling at the kitchen's stench, I manage to fend, "Thanks, but no."

Although she rarely prepares meals, she's amassed thousands of cookbooks that fill a floor-to-ceiling bookshelf that's wedged sideways, to partially block access between her living room and kitchen.

Had her penchant been limited to books, her home might be livable, but here's a partial list of the rest of her stash: she has phonograph records by the thousands, as well as heaps of videos, audio cassettes and CD's; a veritable mountain of computer software claims half a guest room; and computer manuals, along with old computers, are interspersed throughout. Several dozen radios and boxes of radio parts also compete for space. One of several carport sheds is solely devoted to tools; apparently, she's never used any of them. Another shed contains craft materials, fabric remnants, beads, and board games, all with original plastic wrap intact. Her bedroom is also jammed with, as she puts it, "Stuff I've never bothered to deal with."

Shoes, hats, gloves, scarves, purses, tote bags, assorted clothing—price tags dangling—fill the space where I presume a bed resides. With clothing sizes ranging from 10 to 24, Patty, who tips the scales at 240 pounds, is loath to divest of any of them, as she chronically intends to slim down. Also, she's kept every pair of eyeglasses she's ever owned, and then some...a whole lot of them!

Although she's never smoked, she has a sizable collection of ashtrays. Dearest to her heart, however, is her cat paraphernalia—Garfield the Cat is a particular favorite—and so kitty toys and silly cat ceramics abound. Interspersed throughout are cartoons from the Garfield comic strip that she clips and saves daily.

Patty has dozens of pairs of scissors for every imaginable function—ergonomic ones, those for cutting hair, scissors for manicures and pedicures, fabric pinking sheers, and a special pair for trimming eyebrows. Although unable to cook, as mentioned, she owns every kitchen appliance known to humankind, but hasn't the foggiest idea how to use most of them.

"I have this thing for mirrors. Check it out…" We clamber over piles, and laboriously make our way. "Ta-da!" Proudly she shimmies aside so I can peek.

I behold the bathroom wall, which is graced with antiqued stick-on mirror squares. "I love to have mirrors in every room," Patty gushes, "but given the lack of wall space, they're pretty darn useless. Silly me, though, I keep collecting them anyway. A bunch of my favorites are stashed away in boxes. Others, I stack against walls.

"Oh…and I just started collecting beer mirrors. You know, the kind that say Anheuser Busch, or Pabst. Man, I sure *do* love beer!" she chortles. "I also like beer steins and all beer-related paraphernalia."

Several file cabinets overflow with news clippings pertaining to a vast array of topics that have briefly arrested Patty's interest. Stacked atop these cabinets are box-upon-box of photos with images that include family, friends, and a surprising bevy of complete strangers. "I'm ridiculously sentimental," she explains, "and went through a phase, where I took photos of everyone I met. Never mind that I didn't catch their names, I simply craved to memorialize them.

"I also keep pictures of celebrities and movie stars that I admire. Sorry to say, but I recently tossed out those of Roseanne Barr. I used to think we were a lot alike, but then she had all that plastic surgery and turned real fake. Besides, her voice started to grate, and mine is so much lovelier!"

Back outside, Patty rummages through yet another shed to unearth a binder filled with handwriting samples. "I amassed these," she says, "thinking I'd try to master handwriting analysis, but nothing ever came of it."

She hauls over an immense trunk, springs the latches, and juggling paraphernalia, as well as magician materials, spill forth. Latches are flipped to yet another trunk, this one is full of martial arts equipment and dance videos. "This here was yet another of my detours. Seeking to stay mentally fit, I like to challenge myself to achieve new skills." Exercise equipment fills the next shed. "I'm pretty sure," she jokes with a roll of the eyes, "that I'm exercise intolerant."

As she regales me with story after story as to how she came upon and why she values certain items, I find her highly engaging. The reasons she gives for collecting particular objects and the value she ascribes to them tend to vary.

Phone receiver and coiled cord held aloft, with the rest of the telephone missing, she recounts, "Found this on the ground as I entered the pharmacy;

it was the day I met Bernice. She's Asian, works in a hotel and had fascinating stories about the rooms she's cleaned and the celebrities she's met. Oh…I could've listened for hours! She reminds me of a girl I went to school with named Betty, whom we called Bet. So you see, I can't get rid of this, because I don't want to forget either one of them."

Returned to the house, we shuffle through the entryway where numerous bags containing purchases she's never bothered to open are piled; yet again, many of them still have price tags intact. "These are gifts for family and friends. I buy them ahead of time to be sure I have them at the ready, should the need arise."

As we crab-walk about, navigating sideways, traversing mounds, fumbling our way past chest-high towers of magazines and boxes, Patty chatters away, steadily. "I'd like to write about my life, but doing so might exacerbate my carpal tunnel. I thought voice recognition software might make it easier to tell my story, but heaven knows where that equipment's gone.

"Hmm," she cogitates. "I might've packed it away to make room for the recliner."

I scan about; any recliner present is undetectable beneath the junk, but I *do* spot a remarkably tidy corner, replete with printer, scanner and fax, and turn to eye her, quizzical.

"I'm afraid if I hook it up," she admits, "that I'll waste paper. When I finally do get it up and running, I also plan to buy a digital camera, so I can sell some of my books and collectibles on eBay."

Good old eBay, I smile to myself—*the hoarder's pimp and enabler!*

In anticipation of an upcoming bonanza, Patty has collected free advertising art—including cardboard poster ads pertaining to cigarettes and drink: *Absolut Vodka*, *Got Milk*, and *Joe Camel* are some that she eagerly unearthed to display. "Advertising art is all the rage. Really, it's one of the hottest collectibles. A poster like this sells for $2 or $3 on eBay. A few nights ago, I noticed the site offered 55,000 similar kinds of posters for sale, and they're *so* easy to ship by mail!"

All this booty, and so much more, is crammed within the single-wide mobile home she's dubbed the Packrat Aversion Therapy Center.

By her own admission, having so much stuff adversely impacts her life in myriad ways. Once, she had a busy social life, took classes, and participated in church activities. She loved to cook and to entertain, but guests failed to reciprocate and made excuses.

"So then I figured, since I never have visitors, why keep the place clean or bother tidying up? Also, several people I thought were my friends, stole from me. The last guy ripped off my car, took a bunch of money, and absconded with what little valuable jewelry I had. Sorry to say so, but I'm now bitter and paranoid, and no longer trust anyone."

"Thanks to an abundance of insults," as she puts it, "and after a series of mortifying scenes and rejections, I've developed a social phobia."

"When young, I collected men and interesting experiences," Patty confesses. "I always had a husband or lover. We took amazing vacations and had wild adventures, but as I've aged and gotten fat, I no longer attract men. I'm pretty sure that's why I started collecting whole-hog. My books, cats, TV, and the Internet are my passions now."

Despite social isolation and fears that the heavily-laden floor might cave in or that the Health Department or the landlord might evict her, Patty keeps right on accumulating.

△△ △

Much of the clutter Patty attributes to depression, as well as to physical impairments that include a bad back and arthritis. Added to this, lack of energy after a day's work at her temp job leaves her unmotivated. "When I get home, I like to watch TV, drink beer, and write in my journal, which means my life's pretty dull.

"Did I mention my Internet addiction? I'm actually thankful there's no man in my life; I'd be torn between the guy and surfing the Net."

A while back, Patty took a tumble. With all 250 pounds of her weight torqued onto her left ankle, she severed a ligament and smashed her tibia. As a result, a metal strip and screws were inserted to bind the fibula.

Surviving on a minuscule Social Security check, along with a small work-related pension and the occasional temp job, with no way to pay the unreimbursable portion of her hospital bill, thwarting medical advice, she went home via taxi. Alas, as she exited the vehicle, she fell again.

Finding herself unable to get back up, she began to crawl. Ashamed to have neighbors glimpse inside her house, she then hailed a poor passerby and implored him to carve a path to her bed. With no room to maneuver a walker or wheelchair, she had to hobble about.

Turns out, Patty's health insurance *did* pay for the bulk of her hospital expenses, but then declined to cover in-home assistance. "So," she recounts, "I spent dozens of hours seeking volunteer help from various community resources, but came up with nothing. Then I finally called my so-called friends, none responded."

Help arrived when a neighbor, with whom she'd barely spoken, brought coffee each morning, a sandwich at noon, and hot meal for dinner. "This gal was an outstanding cook, but she tended to hurry in, then leave without saying much. She'd been in my house back when it was neat and tidy, and I figured she now had plenty to report back to other neighbors. Oh, she's goodhearted and generous, but is also a vicious gossip."

"As if I didn't have enough headaches." Patty squinches her face. "Several weeks after my accident, the park manager stopped by to ask what I planned to do with the stuff on the porch. He called it a 'stupendous eyesore.' A day later, I received a warning from the Health Department; they say my junk poses a vermin and fire hazard. So I promised to take care of it as soon as my cast came off, but haven't yet done so. Now, I'm terrified that the manager or the County will evict me.

"I tell you"—she pats my arm—"I'm like that guy, you know…Job, in the Bible. Add insult to injury, just as my health improved, a swarm of mice ran roughshod through my place. Nested in boxes and in the trash, with their poop smears blackening my countertops, shelves, and floors, I joked that they were my new pets. Really, it was kinda comical seeing them perform their theatrics! They ran up pull-cords, climbed walls, hung from the drapes, and swan-dove into boxes.

"At first, I was reluctant to put out poison because of my cats, but ended up covering the bait with wire, and then set it in baskets to keep my babies from getting at it. As a result, dead, rotting mice were everywhere. It took a while, but I eventually got that nastiness under control.

"Curiously, due to my leg cast, it had been months since I'd been out and about to acquire more stuff, so when it got removed, my craving to shop seemed to have diminished. Figuring I might be cured of collecting, I decided to get my house in order.

"First off, I tackled the kitchen; it hadn't been tidied in years. Trying to clean was such a joke, though. Due to my arthritic hands and carpal tunnel, I constantly dropped things. Spilling and breaking happens so often, it's hard to clear the debris. I also have trouble gripping the broom and bending down. One day's work, I *did* manage to remove three big bags of rotting food."

"I'm still at it, though." Patty did a pirouette, spun, then took a modest bow. "I find the work tolerable if I give myself one bite-size task each day. Even then, I get overwhelmed and discouraged. Yet, I try not to overdo and start with a fresh attitude come morning. As a result, there's been a smidgen of progress.

"At times, I backslide, buying stuff I can't afford and have no place to stash. The goal that I've kept, though, I take out at least one bag a day. How do I remove it from the house, you may ask? I fill it up, not too heavy, mind you, toss it down the hall to the living room, then out the front door. Sometimes I'm so winded, I ask a passing stranger to carry the bag to the dumpster."

As I nod encouragingly, the image of emptying a swimming pool a single eye-dropper full at a time comes to mind.

"Hours on end," Patty continues, "I try to sort through papers, but get overwhelmed. See...this is how I work." She picks through a pile of news clippings. "I plan to give these articles on communication to my pharmacy clerk who says her teenage daughter won't talk to her."

She lifts a brown envelope from an immense paper pile. "This particular bunch is from a phone company who claims to offer better service, so I can't toss this until I check the details."

Amazingly, she reveals empty kitchen cupboard and drawer space. "If I put dishes and papers away," she discloses, "I forget that they exist." If the folder with the phone company's prices gets filed away, she fears she'll forget about it, as well.

As she carefully examines each item, Patty appears incapable of determining its significance or what gives it importance, relative to other objects. Recently I'd learned this wasn't uncommon. Every decision made as to what to save has to do with its intended future use. Ironically, given the myriad of piles, nothing's easily accessible for her to re-examine anyway. So even crumpled, blank scraps are kept, lest she run out of writing paper.

Patty's face contorts as she contemplates tossing out a ragged T-shirt. The effort of decision-making seems megalithic as she cuddles and examines it, then drifts into a long, convoluted anecdote as to how it came to be acquired. Losing track of sorting altogether and overwhelmed by the effort, shirt dropped in the saving pile, she pauses to take a break.

I've just witnessed a process known as *churning*, which involves busily moving objects around, yet not getting rid of, or accomplishing a thing. This *churning* is related to the particular difficulties hoarders have making decisions.

Patty *does* attempt to recycle by giving junk to friends or by donating to thrift stores. Inevitably, when she drops donations off at the Goodwill, she takes a look around, and cannot resist buying more.

"Yesterday, I paid my favorite thrift store a visit, giving myself five minutes inside to drop stuff off," she announces as she resumes sorting, "then I spotted a familiar face, got to gabbing and ended up staying at least two hours; it's the only way I socialize."

"I try to be selective and to justify my purchases, but when I enter certain stores, like I did yesterday, I snap into this hypnotic trance. It's particularly bad when I see books. Despite my lack of space, and the fact that I'll never read them, I returned home with five grocery bags full of books."

When able to drive again, she began to attend group therapy. "Though the members are in the same boat as I am," Patty recounts, "and have houses full of junk, none will admit to having a hoarding disorder. All of them seem anxious and depressed, but I'm not sure any are suicidal, so I didn't discuss my attempts to take my life, or my many hospitalizations. Really, my main goal being there is to get my Paxil renewed. It lifts my spirits and reduces my anxiety, but unfortunately doesn't impact my collecting.

"One poor woman in the group is an obsessive-compulsive who fears contamination, so she washes and scrubs, till her hands blister up. Lest anyone touche her stuff, she goes nuts, hollers and panics, then deems it dirty. She even covers her handbag in plastic wrap and wears gloves to touch everything.—Whew, I'm thankful I don't have that problem!

"The public needs to know that folks like us aren't lazy or deliberately messy," Patty continues. "Most of us have a chemical imbalance. Believe me, living this way is no piece of cake. Without proper medication and cognitive behavioral therapy, it's impossible to manage. Until science finds a better solution, I take my pills and cooperate by attending therapy. Mostly, though, I pray that someday my life will become manageable."

⌂⌂ ⌂

Unlike most hoarders, Patty had insight into her problem. Yet, despite her best intentions, she's unable to cease collecting. As a result, her life continues to burgeon out of control.

"As I look around at these piles and notice the filth, I agonize," she confides. "My mind screams and races; I'm so overwhelmed. Sometimes, I pray that I die in my sleep. But then I worry what might happen to my cats. Nobody loves them as I do."

Raised Christian, after delving into other religions she now deems herself a mystic, and garners solace through the teachings of Religious Science and Buddhist meditation. She's even cleared space in her bedroom for an altar. A brass bell, shimmery scarf, offerings of fruit and rice, and a cherubic fellow's photo are artfully arranged atop it.

Despite numerous challenges, she manages to find an upside, "I'm terribly lonely, but am glad my depression is finally under control, and that I have a sense of humor about my situation. And, heck, I'm relieved that I'm not a compulsive counter, or a checker, or that I fear contamination. It would be unbearably awful to have obsessive thoughts—imagine thinking, over and over, that you've harmed someone!"

"I hold onto happy times, routinely say affirmations, and tell myself to stop with the negative ruminations. For example, I envision myself as more attractive and that I've grown thinner, to the point that I can wear size twelve dresses again. Surely, all the boxes I heft help me slim down. I visualize having a tidy, lovely home, and that I find loving, kind friends. Someday, I'm certain, all of it will manifest."

Lest the reader feel exhausted from hearing this narrative, that's precisely the point; to grasp the convoluted and tortured world inhabited by a classic hoarder, where having stuff begets more stuff, which leads to myriad social, economic and health challenges. The problems hoarders face isn't merely about their junk, it's about a life gone to the dogs.

CHAPTER 2

Clutter Busters Strike Again— The Business of Cleanup

"Insanity is doing the same thing over and over and expecting different results."

—Variously attributed to Einstein, Freud, and Maya Angelou.

My ad in the local paper read thus: ***Clutter Buster: Professional Organizer***
 Do chaos, clutter, and crowded closets confound your life?
 If so, I help you toss out, minimize, then reorganize your home, office, garage, basement or attic. By maintaining an ordered work or living space, you reduce

stress and save money, energy, and time.—*Call William, your professional organizer.*

Many wonder what grants me the credentials to be called a Professional Organizer and to therefore turn a stranger's house upside down. Certainly no college or home accreditation course offers *Mess Management 101*. What *does* add to my cred is that I'm big, somewhat intimidating, and naturally bossy.

While planning our year-end sixth grade class party, my friend's mom asked her son how the event was getting organized, to which he replied, "We get together and Bill (William) tells us what to do."

My decidedly recessive shopping gene manifests as an aversion to shopping malls as well as department stores, and my spiritual life eschews amassing an abundance of worldly goods, so both factors add to my resumé. Also, I've moved often enough to embody the axiom *a rolling stone gathers no moss* and have ruthlessly winnowed my possessions down to bare essentials, which gives me a modicum of authority to encourage, coax, and cajole others to do likewise.

Although my habits of tidiness and organization exhibited at an early age, I don't recall being overly anal. I wasn't fastidious in my dress or appearance, and my bedroom drawers and school desk were ever a-jumble.

Once a year, though, an urge descended—typically on a Sunday, so perhaps orderliness *is* next to Godliness—to thoroughly clean my bedroom. Dust became smears on paper towels, the vacuum probed the nether-reaches beneath the bed, and the closet and drawers got organized, ship-shape. Later that night, I'd slip between fresh sheets, glance about my immaculate room, and bask with perverse pleasure.

When asked what I wanted to be as and adult, it's not like I replied, "Maybe a fireman, a doctor, or no, wait...a professional organizer!"

My clutter-busting career didn't coalesce until much later, while sharing a friend's Massachusetts home. In exchange for room and board, I tended his garden a specific number of hours. Yet, this arrangement was impossible to fulfill in the deep snows of winter. As a result, I cleaned and tidied my pal's immense basement, consolidating similar items such as light bulbs, paint cans,

Christmas decorations, and tools together. Sometime later, as I organized yet another friend's home office, I realized that I had a knack for it.

So when I moved back to San Francisco, in a moment of curiosity I discovered half-a-dozen listings in the Yellow Pages (remember them?) under the section titled, *Professional Organizers*. Coincidentally, I then bumped into a friend who mentioned he'd been exploring the same line of work, and he suggested we attend a meeting of the National Association of Professional Organizers (NAPO).

A week later, I found myself at a gathering of seventy people—all women, but for four men (curiously, all were gay)—and, as one might imagine, the meeting was *very* organized. One fifteen-year clutter-buster veteran specialized in corporate organizing. Another's niche involved assisting families to prepare for the death of an ill or elderly loved one. Most attendees, however, turned out to be run of the mill, clean 'em up, toss 'em out task-masters like me.

⌂⌂ ⌂

Founded in 1985, the NAPO has morphed into a booming business, and boasts a burgeoning membership world-wide. As a not-for-profit association whose mission is to promote professional organizers, these people connect those in need with appropriate resources to help them get organized.

The NAPO has its own professional code of ethics and takes itself very seriously. As a result, they want their clients. as well as the public at large to do likewise. Integrity, competence and respect, while maintaining strict confidentiality, are requisite with this group. Furthermore, organizers must agree to only offer services in areas for which they are qualified. Colaborative support with other NAPO colleagues is integral to their charter, and members strive to be taken seriously.

With a strong commitment to ethics and ongoing education, the group has established professional standards, along with specific knowledge-based requirements that include certification and ongoing continuing education for the professional organizer. Organizers must complete 1,500 hours of paid client work over a three year interval to be eligible to apply for their certification exam. These hours may include, but are not limited to: on-site organizing, coaching, consulting, virtual organizing, participation in interactive workshops. and the training of clients as well as fellow organizers. Feng-shui—the Chinese system of establishing harmony with one's environment—involves evaluation of a home in metaphoric terms for the presence of "invisible forces" that bind the universe, earth, and humanity together (commonly known as chi), and is also deemed by the NAPO as an accredited skill.[1]

When Tammy set out to hire a professional organizer to help straighten up her home office, she checked out the Institute For Challenging Disorganization's Clutter-Hoarding Scale. Relieved to discover that her messiness hadn't reached the hoarding stage, their scale describes five levels of messiness, which are determined by the conditions within one's home.

The Level One home is considered to be messy; while there is some clutter, everything works and all the rooms and exits are usable. At the other end of the spectrum, the Level Five home is unsafe for habitation and may require the services of a specially trained professional organizer, as well as intervention from government agencies such as Code Enforcement, the Public Guardian, Adult Protective Services (APS), along with police and fire departments. As it turns out, Tammy's office is considered to be a Level One, meaning she can hire a professional organizer who has no special training.

Encouraged by my first NAPO meeting, I placed ads in several local rags, including church and synagogue newsletters. Then slowly, by word of mouth, my business took off.

My plan of organizing was this: one pile for the garbage bin; one for the Goodwill—if the client hasn't worn/used/tasted it within a year, it's a goner; one pile for items to return or to give to family and friends; and the rest of the stuff was kept. Negotiations were permitted but generally my bossiness prevailed.

When a stalemate was reached, into the *Maybe* box the item went. For the terminally indecisive, typically that box overflowed. As a fail-safe, if my client failed to use or think about an article in that *Maybe* box over the next six months, it went to the Goodwill.

Ultimately, it wasn't up to me to decide what to keep and what to toss. In essence, I served as moral support—a cattle prod, if you will—to keep up the momentum. Clients, I found, who spent years amassing tended to avoid organizing and parting with their stuff, and inevitably found any old excuse to delay a tad longer.

With avoidance and justifications abounding, I once found my employer hunched over a shoebox. Full-to-overflowing with thousands of business cards, he frantically sorted through to salvage those most important. Repeatedly, another client retreated to the kitchen to ingest yet another little snack. One woman insisted she call her sister for permission to give away a purple jacket she'd received as a gift some thirty-five years prior. Although I assured her that the sibling couldn't give a flying hoot, she rang up the sister anyhow.

As clients divest their stuff, emotions arise. With one woman who was splitting up with her husband, I acted more as therapist than trash ejector, as she was as delicate as a hothouse flower. While boxing up volumes of birdwatching books with another fellow, I happened upon a photograph of two dapper men who appeared to be in their 40s: one was my client in his younger years, the other I surmised to be his life-partner.

When we started in on the wardrobe closet, with tears brimming, the fellow gripped a pair of mahogany oxfords to his heart. It had been five years since his beloved's death and he was now ready to dispose of his worldly goods. As a result, I set aside my cattle prod, backed off, and acted more gentle after that.

Several times I've been outfoxed. After working hard the day prior, I returned to one job to find my remorseful protegé in the dumpster, busily tossing out it's contents and carting everything back to the house.

Jettisoning clutter can open life to the unexpected. When Lance cleared his home, he met his future wife shortly thereafter. In the process of clearing, another fellow came across a vintage book which he sold for a whopping $30,000, which enabled him to then take several months off work to live it up. When Patty from Chapter One eventually cleared her home, she found she had a knack for organizing and became a clutter-buster herself.

In addition to the NAPO, other forms of support exist. "Banish all clutter and find inner peace," enjoins the perky Marla Cilley. Known to her devoted followers as The FlyLady, Cilley sponsors a quirky web-site that inserts a bit of fun into the cleaning and organizing process. Seekers of inner joy and a clutter-free life sign on to receive her daily uplifting directive. So, as I read Cilley's 27 Fling Boogie Challenge, I had a good chuckle. "Grab a plastic bag," she enjoins, "run through the house, and find precisely 27 objects to toss out."[2]

Not to be outdone, Sandra Felton runs the *Messies Anonymous* web-site. As an advocate of The Mount Vernon Cleaning Method, Felton imparts tidbits as to how the staff at Mount Vernon manages to keep the national memorial ship-shape. *Don't overdo; pace yourself; work with a time limit; take a day off each week so you have something to look forward to; reward yourself when you overcome a big hurdle*—are a few of her offerings.[3]

Some agencies specialize in the cleanup of trash houses. One such organization, Peninsula Community Service, is a nonprofit that offers a drop-in support group for hoarders as well as the chronically disorganized. Alan Merrifield, the group's founder, often works in tandem with government officials, conservators, realtors, property owners, as well as tenants to clean up residential properties.

Merrifield is acutely attuned to the hoarder's feelings because he, too, is one. While he relies on his wife to keep his own inclinations in check, many others lack such support. As we talk by phone, he recalls one job, "I have no idea how, but each morning this couple who lived in a jam-packed house, carved a means of getting out so they could use the restroom at a nearby Denny's to freshen up. After, they'd go back and re-seal themselves inside.

"In addition to all the junk inside," he continues, "there was a whole lot of kitty crap. What little floor was exposed had been covered, several inches deep, with cat litter, which prevented all the doors from swinging any direction. Their kitchen roof sported a large hole through which the cats came and went. To make a long story short, we emptied the house with the husband's acquiescence, only to find that it was in such bad shape that it had to be bulldozed. A new home was built the next year, and they seemed pretty happy, but who knows if they've gone back to collecting...."

Merrifield recounts yet another tale: Maddie, hadn't been seen by neighbors in some time, so the authorities were called to check on her. "When the rescue team knocked on her door, she didn't answer. So around the back they went to pound on the kitchen door and holler. When she failed to respond, firetrucks were called, One fella broke a window, let himself in, then had to work his way through to the front to let the others inside. Trash, litter, and a tremendous stench filled the place, but there was no sign of Maddie. As best they could, they continued to look about, and kept calling for her.

"Finally, someone spotted a leg jutting out from a pile and grabbed it. And, well, Maddie screamed and jumped up, yelling that they'd invaded her privacy. Later, when we got to know her, she confessed such mortification that she'd hid, too embarrassed to face anyone.

"In addition to hoarding," Merrifield continues, "Maddie had a problem with incontinence, but her doctor declined to operate until she lost weight. With friends and family no longer in touch, her despair reached its zenith. That's when Peninsula Community Services got involved."

With help, her house got cleared and cleaned, and then we helped Maddie stage a garage sale. It was during that event that she met her neighbors and made new friends. Buoyed by the attention, she eventually lost weight, underwent that bladder surgery, regained a social life, and even made plans to invite her long lost brother for dinner.

"Truly, a likable woman," Merrifield recalls, "folks began to drop in just to see how she fared. Last time I saw her, she stopped by my garage sale. And no, she didn't buy a thing, but she *did* seem pretty darn happy."

Merrifield's advice to hoarders: "You need to know that you aren't alone and that help is available for the asking. A lot of people share the same tendencies that hoarders struggle with to one degree or another, so it can be lifesaving to have support. I know, because I'm one of those people."

CHAPTER 3

Animals do it, Humans do it—A Brief History of Hoarding

One asks which is more damaging to modern humanity: the thirst for money or consuming haste...in either case, fear plays a very important role: fear of being overtaken by one's competitors, the fear of becoming poor, the fear of making wrong decisions, or of not being up to snuff....

—Konrad Lorenz.

ANIMALS DO IT, HUMANS DO it; even the dearly departed—although it's unlikely they give a damn—aren't exempt from the proclivity to collect and hoard. Ancient Egyptians lavishly filled tombs with the flotsam and jetsam of everyday life, for they figured such items to be essential for their disincarnate existence. For example in China, when thousands of life-size terracotta horses and soldiers were unearthed, they seemed intent upon marching into eternity with their Emperor Qin.

Archaeologists who excavated his tomb were astounded to find replicas of his vast army that included clay war implements, horses, and chariots. Rather than adhere to the custom of the times, namely burying the army alive in order to accompany their ruler into the afterlife, he so kindly insisted they merely inter life-size statues.

Twenty two hundred years ago, this Emperor, perhaps the first to promulgate the axiom, "He who dies with the most toys wins," practically swallowed up the world. As owner of 270 palaces, he conquered all surrounding kingdoms and then declared himself first Emperor of China. Quite the innovator, he built roads, irrigation canals, and The Great Wall. He also standardized laws, established weights and measures, created a form of currency, and formalized the use of written characters. While not a hoarder by today's' definition, he certainly managed to accomplish and to amass a whole lot in his lifetime!

The term *hoarding* has it's mundane origins in the Old English word, *collecting*. Collecting appears in the legend of King Midas, a tale about a miserly fellow who fatefully ends up aggregating straw, instead of gold. In this instance, hoarding connotes one man's fruitless efforts to conserve inherently worthless materials. Nowadays, this fable also applies to successful individuals who busily fill their lives with riches, then suddenly realize that all the wealth in the world cannot bring them peace of mind.

Apropos the conversion of straw into gold, hoarding is seen by some as a way to meet basic needs, as well as a means of self-nurturing. Additionally for some, the possession of a lot of stuff creates the illusion of power and control

According to Dr. Randy Frost, compulsive hoarding is defined as: "The acquisition of, and the failure to discard possessions, which appear to be useless or of limited value."[1] The word "acquisition" is significant, for not only do hoarders have trouble deciding what to discard, they also acquire massive amounts of redundant items by shopping, scavenging, and occasionally by stealing. The hoarder's inability to part with his or her stuff may stem from sentiment or from so-called practical considerations or, may even be the result of delusional illogic. Ultimately, incessant acquisition fills up the home to create cramped and squalid living conditions.

Initially, it was conjectured that most hoarders commonly experienced massive deprivation, such as the Holocaust or The Great Depression. Such individuals never know when the very thing they've tossed out might be needed to save their life, so according to their mindset, the most prudent strategy is to save everything.

During my tenure as a professional organizer, most of my clients were well-to-do, which prompted me to wonder if hoarding predominantly manifests among the wealthy. Although the acquisitive Howard Hughes and Randolph Hearst enjoyed extreme wealth, I soon found that hoarding crossed socioeconomic lines and didn't necessarily result from an impoverished upbringing.

Then again, we've all seen street people shoving shopping carts, full to the brim with who knows what. Perhaps the main difference between the rich and poor is that the wealthy possess the means to acquire using credit cards, and can afford to shop in boutiques. Many middle-class folks shop online, or at Bed, Bath and Beyond, as well as at Macy's. These people may also frequent Wal-Mart or peruse Amazon, and plenty of them enjoy watching the Shopping Channel. The less affluent snap up flea market and thrift store finds, while the impoverished street lady gathers from trash bins and thinks nothing of dumpster-diving.

As it turns out, hoarding isn't limited to Anglo-American cultures. A few cross-cultural studies conducted in Egypt, Italy, and Australia show that hoarding is, indeed, a universal phenomenon that crosses ethnic, gender, and economic boundaries.

"It seems economics doesn't have much to do with acquisition or saving," explains Gail Steketee, hoarding researcher, "although those with money may purchase more expensive items (e.g.: the compulsive purchase of designer clothes) than those who might collect free or inexpensive objects (e.g., papers, plastic containers, tag sale items). The manner in which people collect things varies due to different cultural mechanisms for how possessions are available. For example, in the USA, yard sales and used clothing stores serve as common sources for acquiring, but this is rare in a place like Italy."²

As we saw, Patty from Chapter One has a passion for books. This obsessive aggregation happens to be the only hobby with an illness named for it, and is termed *bibliomania*. Bibliomaniacs hoard ideas and thoughts that have been committed to word. *Biblioholism* involving the excessive longing for, and the acquisition of books, as well as other reading materials, isn't relegated to the exclusive purview of eggheads and intellectuals.

Who among us doesn't hold onto the occasional magazine, newspaper, pile of books, or mail, including e-mail? Throughout literate human history, language, in its written form, has been critical, for it serves as proof that we exist.

Ralph Ellis, Jr. began collecting ornithological books at the age of 15. When his penchant threatened to exhaust the family estate, his mother had him committed to a sanitarium. Diagnosed as mentally ill, but not insane—whatever that means—within a couple years he was finally released. Back at it again, he proceeded to load up two freight cars with 65,000 volumes of reading material, and headed back to his native New York.³

Then there's the notorious bibliomaniac Stephen Blumberg, who managed to plunder twenty million rare books from libraries across North America. At some point, a certain Mafia Don inquired why Blumberg didn't devote himself to the theft of valuables the likes of precious metals or jewels. Blumberg retorted that he didn't steal books to sell or to read, but absconded for the sheer pleasure of possessing them. Taking Blumberg for a mere crackpot, the mobster swiftly lost interest. Yet in 1990, authorities caught up with the book thief and found his Iowa home stacked, floor to ceiling, with nine tons of books, 23,600 in all.⁴

Books aside, how about that foot fetishist Imelda Marcos, who amassed a shoe collection of several thousand pairs? Then there's singer Elton John, who converted his mansion attic to display his massive collection of sunglasses.

Filled with inexplicable oddities, including stairs that lead nowhere, there's The Winchester Mystery House in San Jose, CA. Built by Sarah Winchester, Winchester Rifle heiress, ongoing construction of the home posed a massive lifelong undertaking. Believing herself to be haunted by thousands of souls who died as a result of the rifle's manufacture, Sarah Winchester followed advice gleaned from a spiritual séance, which went something like this: as long as building construction was underway, she appeased the restless spirits, thereby enabling her to live on, ad infinitum.

Intended to keep death at bay, she perpetually added on, until her home, spanned 24,000 square feet over a space of 6 acres, and numbered 160 rooms. These days, the grounds and mansion are open to the public, and boast 2000 doors, 2000 windows, 47 fireplaces, 40 stairways, 13 bathrooms, 6 kitchens, 3 elevators, 2 basements, and 40 bedrooms.

Regardless, Sarah Winchester did, indeed succumb.

Perhaps the most infamous case of hoarding is that of the Collyer brothers of New York. Homer and Langley Collyer, both exceptionally bright men, attended Columbia University, where Homer obtained a degree in admiralty law and Langley studied engineering as well as chemistry. Langley, also a concert pianist, played professionally and performed at Carnegie Hall.

Lifelong bachelors, the two shared the Fifth Avenue brownstone they'd inherited from their mother. For a time, they seemed normal, had an ordinary social life, entertained, and left home on a regular basis. Homer practiced maritime law, while Langley worked as a piano dealer. With a passion to invent, Langley enjoyed tinkering and managed to invent a device to vacuum the innards of pianos and also adapted a Model T Ford to generate electricity.

Life changed abruptly in 1933, when Homer lost his eyesight, prompting Langley to quit work to care for him. When Homer then became paralyzed due to inflammatory rheumatism, both men eschewed medical care, asserting that, as sons of a physician, and given their medical library of 15,000 books, they possessed all necessary information needed to treat and cure Homer.

Set about to restore Homer's eyesight through diet and rest, Langley enjoined his sibling to consume a hundred oranges per week, along with black bread and peanut butter—foods he claimed held curative powers for blindness. Highly optimistic as to his ministrations, Langley's retort to the query of a news reporter regarding the vast amounts of reading materials that filled the house was as follows, "I am saving newspapers for Homer, so when he regains his sight he can catch up on the news."

When the Depression hit, their largely affluent neighborhood went into decline. Whites moved out of the area, and the brothers saw crime and poverty surge as increasing numbers of African-Americans moved in. As a result, both men came to fear the changing demographic of their neighborhood.

Thereafter, Langley turned paranoid, only venturing out under cover of darkness to walk the streets. Picking edibles from the trash, he begged food from grocers, then returned home to share the booty with his brother. During these forays, he also managed to scrounge and cart home myriad kinds of trash.

With rumors abounding, the brothers came to wider attention in 1938 when a story about them appeared in *The New York Times*. Addressing their penchant for hoarding, the piece also made mention of rumors that the brothers lived in "Orientalist splendor" and that they sat upon vast piles of cash. As imagined, this tidbit was precisely the publicity the two men dreaded and sought to avoid.

After several subsequent burglary attempts, Langley applied his considerable smarts to create a vast, complex maze of tunnel systems, then rigged the tunnels with trip-wires, meant to send an avalanche of garbage cascading down upon intruders. The brothers then ensconced themselves in "nests" created throughout the floor-to-ceiling debris.

In 1947, a tipster reported that a horrid stench emanated from the home, which then prompted emergency responders to break in through a second-story window. Lo and behold, looming before them stood a massively solid wall of junk. This wall included newspapers, folding beds, chairs, a sewing machine, untold numbers of packages and bundles, a baby carriage, and parts of a wine press. To gain access, the authorities were forced to remove the obstructing wall by tossing the debris onto the street below.

Several hours later, by following the smell, they managed to locate the body of Homer Collyer in an alcove, surrounded by boxes piled to the ceiling. Medical examiners later confirmed that he'd died of starvation and heart disease.

When the doting Langley failed to appear at Homer's funeral, it was suspected that he'd predeceased his brother. As a result, law enforcement returned to the scene in an attempt to find him.

In the search, they removed numerous outdated phone registries, a horse's jawbone, a Steinway piano, as well as fourteen grand pianos, an x-ray machine, and assorted materials from the father's medical practice, including pickled human organs. Eight live cats were found, while other excavated items included baby carriages, rusty bicycles, rotted food, several potato peelers, a gun collection, chandeliers, bowling balls, camera equipment, a sawhorse, several dressmaking dummies, numerous portraits, photos of pinup-girls from the early 1900s, plaster busts, Mrs. Collyer's hope chest, and several rusty bed springs. Over 25,000 books—as mentioned, thousands pertaining to medicine—along with others about engineering, and law, were also unearthed.

Tapestries, along with hundreds of yards of silk and other fabrics came out of the rubble. There were clocks, a clavichord, two organs, several banjos, as well as violins, bugles, accordions, a gramophone, and vinyl records. Countless bundles of newspapers and magazines, some decades old, were also excavated. Thousands of bottles and tin cans, along with mountains of plain old trash also came from the rubble.

How Langley managed to haul the bulk of a horse-drawn carriage inside, as well as the chassis of a Model-T Ford, is beyond imagining. In all, cleaners removed 120 tons of junk.

At last, they found Langley's body a mere ten feet from where his brother met his demise. Police theorize that as he crawled through a two-foot wide tunnel, lined with rusty bed springs and chests of drawers to bring food to Homer, he inadvertently tripped one of his own booby traps and got crushed by tumbled debris.[5]

Modern day firefighters refer to a hoarder's dwelling as a *Collyer Mansion* or merely as a *Collyer*—meaning a house so full of trash and debris that it's a serious danger to its occupants.

As if to emulate those Ancient Egyptians, Langley and the hapless, disabled Homer effectively entombed themselves within tons of amassed booty. And so, Langley's herculean efforts not only personify the adage *You can't take it with you,* but also, in this case, *Your junk just might take you along with it!*

Not only do humans hoard, but a variety of other species, including mammals, insectivores, primates, carnivores, birds, and rodents do so. Yet hoarding in animals, unlike hoarding in humans, mostly serves a practical purpose and encompasses a diverse range of behaviors.

Measured by frequency, including the type and quantity of food collected, along with the materials that animals store, as well as the interval between storing and consumption, animal hoarding involves the creation of caches, or a series of locales, where food is hidden away in order to lather nourish themselves and their offspring.

One creature who most definitely hoards in the interest of propagation is the bowerbird. Among the notable characteristics of this bird are their extraordinarily complex courtship and mating rituals. In and around the bower, the male bowerbird places a variety of brightly colored objects that he's collected. Objects include hundreds of shells, leaves, flowers, feathers, stones, berries, and even discarded plastic items, along with coins, nails, rifle shells, or pieces of glass. Intent upon luring the female, the male spends hours arranging the collection to create an attractive avenue of objects.

Mate-searching females visit multiple bowers, often returning to the same male several times to watch his elaborate courtship displays and to inspect the quality of his assemblage. They even taste the paint placed on the walls. Should the female show interest, the male performs an elaborate dance in an attempt to seduce her.

⌂⌂ ⌂

Despite the extravagant, yet practical displays of the bowerbird, no compulsive hoarding equivalent exists in animals to the extreme that it occurs in humans.

Yet, we still tend to look to animal behaviors for clues regarding our own actions. For example, domesticated female canaries gather up pieces of string placed inside their cages and methodically weave them together to build nests. Female canaries who reside in the wild or in isolation perform nest-building rituals in this same precise manner.

Such behavior, known as *fixed action patterning* is ingrained within all animals of the same species, and is conducted the exact manner for all of them. Austrian zoologist Konrad Lorenz, concludes that *fixed action patterns* are part of instinctive behavioral programming, meaning that evolution has caused information to be stored in the brains of a particular animal species as an integral part of their genetic makeup.

When the Greylag Goose displaces an egg from the nest, it reflexively rolls it back, using its beak to tuck it beneath it's breast. Lorenz found that these birds complete this same action, rolling an imaginary egg, despite removal of the actual egg.

Human examples of *fixed action patterning* include the infant's reflexive gripping of Mama's fingers and one's adrenaline-fueled inclination to run when someone shouts, *Fire!* Even when such actions are irrelevant, humans experience fixed actions while enduring stressful situations.

According to Lorenz, the human mind contains built-in drives that determine what we see and how we react. Similar to certain animals, humans are pattern-making and pattern-repeating creatures. For example, hoarding and collecting behaviors in humans are seen as similar to the bird's nest-building rituals. Originally critical for human survival, our proclivity to gather up and collect is deeply ingrained, which makes our collecting-related behaviors extremely tough to eradicate. If we take a leap, while our modern day proclivity to hoard and collect serves no practical survival purpose, it *does* persist as a throwback to the past.

△△ △

As we know, the term *packrat* is another appellation used to refer to the human hoarder. With regard to the animal kingdom, however, the word actually refers to another living creature—the packrat. This frisky, furry rodent habitually collects material from its environs to store in dens, creating trash piles called *middens*.

Analysis of the contents of ancient packrat middens has enabled scientists to discover types of plant life that existed 40,000 years ago. So, centuries from now anthropologists may unearth our human middens to find rubble that's comprised of Tonka Toys, Starbucks mugs, Rubbermaid storage boxes, and a vast trove of other treasures and then try to ascertain significant details regarding our cultural values.

Acquisitiveness is embedded in our human genes—likely, a vestige of our antecedents' inclination to gather and store dried meat, roots, and berries against times of scarcity. Later this human tendency manifested in the saving of shells, stones, and feathers for adornment and to trade as currency. Yet, modern day hoarding is clearly seen as an evolutionary adaptation gone awry.

But why and how do hoarding behaviors get activated, and what is their significance?

Ethology, come to prominence due to Lorenz's work in the 1930s, studies and compares animal behaviors. As we know, hoarding with regard to the animal kingdom is primarily associated with the collecting and storage of food. Rats, squirrels, beavers, and birds busily gather up foodstuffs, as well as twigs and stones, essential for species survival.

Much like the squirrel's urge to gather and sequester away nuts for winter, hoarders feel helpless to resist their inner urges as well. Akin to the squirrel, who creates a protective, cave-like burrow, the hoarder is beset with an itch to acquire and to keep every scrap of paper that crosses his or her path. Lacking conscious discernment, this individual hauls these materials back to the nest—in this case, their home—and it would seem, then uses those gleanings to burrow in and to insulate.

What was once a practical survival mechanism for humans, now manifests as a useless, but intense, unrelenting quest that's become locked into overdrive. While collecting, stowing and hoarding behaviors served our ancestors well thousands of years ago, such activities now pose a hindrance, and even mark the hoarder as a freakish outcast.

CHAPTER 4

Collector, Packrat, or Hoarder?—It's a Fine Line

---

*"The core of paranoia is the detachment of the libido from objects.
A reverse course is taken by the collector who directs his surplus
libido onto an inanimate object with a love of things."*

—SIGMUND FREUD

FREDERICK CLEGG, A LONELY CLERK, meticulously collects butterflies, but then turns his attention onto the lovely Miranda. Using his talents as curator and collector, this novel's protagonist sets out to possess her. Shedding all semblance of self-control, he spirals into violence that makes the blood run cold.

John Fowles, a major international author, first published Clegg's tale, *The Collector* in 1963. In many ways, this horror story served as the prequel to a whole slew of psychological thrillers involving obsession.

While compulsive hoarding can be a sign of mental illness, as in Clegg's case, it's rare that collectors—although many are solitary and eccentric—are emotionally disturbed. What hoarders and collectors *do* have in common is that they have more possessions than they truly need and many of them find it a challenge to keep stuff organized.

David collects vinyl records and baseball cards and doesn't like to sell, trade, or give any of them away. Overall, he leads a normal life, holds down a job, and his home is relatively tidy. Yet, he also acquires and fails to throw out a large array of other sundry items that have little or no value.

So when does a collector or a packrat cross the line into hoarding?

For some, the words packrat and hoarder are interchangeable. Yet, collectors often fondly use the term packrat with reference to themselves. While I never found clear parameters that differentiate the terms, a packrat may begin as a collector who eventually has so much stuff that life careens out of control. On the other hand, a packrat may be a hard-core collector who permanently resides in the netherworld between collecting and hoarding, yet their pursuits never become unmanageable.

Collectors, packrats and hoarders *do* have one thing in common: They love acquiring things. The kinds of items they collect, along with the stuff's significance and the impact collecting has on their lives, can help to distinguish the avid collector from a packrat, and a packrat from a compulsive hoarder.

△△ △

Abbe, a 49-year-old married businesswoman, readily dubs herself as a packrat. With a love of collecting and restoring vintage quilts, this highly discerning woman spends weekends with her husband, scouring fairs and antique shops in search of that certain special coverlet. Never one to purchase on impulse, she does considerable research ahead of time and if unable to find the perfect addition, departs empty-handed.

However, after devoting three decades to aggregating and restoring American quilts, Abbe's amassed a vast assemblage. To showcase her finds, she's added on to her home, where she neatly displays quilts according to category in designated rooms. On occasion, with great reluctance, she sells a piece to make way for a new purchase.

Then there's Walter, a newly divorced retiree who is also a self-described packrat. Most days, he spends scouring flea markets, garage and estate sales, as well as the occasional dollar store in search of treasure. Friends refer to his so-called precious finds as "garbage," as he tends to amass piles of fliers and newspapers, and claims that he doesn't want them to go to waste.

Walter's tendencies began in his twenties, but after retirement his collecting shifted into overdrive. Nowadays, his home is so jam-packed he can only traverse a small goat trail between the kitchen, bedroom, and bathroom. It's no surprise that some time back, his wife got fed up and departed.

When his remaining friends suggested he clean up his house and even offered to help, he got furious and demanded they leave him alone. Moreover, he rants and rages when his children volunteer to go through boxes and throw out useless stuff. Walter simply cannot fathom parting with anything and fears that if he does, he might lose something of value.

Although Abbe's quilt collection is vast, her finds don't impair her day-to-day function. She efficiently stores or displays her quilts and their presence doesn't consume her home. Additionally, collecting comes in a distant third to family and to her successful business career.

Walter's accumulations, however, have taken on a life of their own. Despite the fact that his existence is in shambles, his compulsion to collect dominates everything. Significantly, he cannot throw out items that most consider garbage. His intense emotional attachment to his junk, along with his lack of insight pose such problems that he's alienated family and friends, to say nothing of the fact that his home is nearly uninhabitable.

Above all, hoarding led to the end of his marriage, alienated his children, and put an end to most friendships. Safe to say, Walter's behavior is consistent with compulsive hoarding, whereas Anne is simply a passionate collector.

Given our pervasively acquisitive culture it can be tough to distinguish between the disorganized collector and the packrat whose hoarding has gone overboard. There are certain circumstances, as we know, including advanced age, poor health, or mental disturbance that can tip the ordinary collector over into hoarding.

According to Randy Frost, "For the person whose collecting has become hoarding, possessions become unorganized piles of clutter that are so large that they prevent rooms from being used for normal activities."[1]

Demarcation between collecting and hoarding might be best determined by how much space a collection occupies. Treasures confined to display shelves, or boxed and kept in closets, thereby leaving the rest of the home functional, don't cross the line. Collections that fill a room or two, with much of the home still intact may also not be excessive. Should that compilation metastasize to take over the house, leaving its occupants little to no space to function, then it's goodbye collector, hello hoarder.

Hoarding is officially diagnosed when acquisition and saving results in clinically significant distress or the downfall of social, occupational, financial, or health-related functions. Impairment may also include the inability to maintain a safe living environment.

Collecting, on the other hand, is defined as the selective gathering and keeping of objects that have subjective value. Attendant activities involve the search for, and acquisition of, a specific category of items. With a focus that includes meticulous care and ardor, collecting is largely seen as a creative act; in part, its an art form.

The hobbyist collector has the opportunity to become expert within a narrowly defined niche, and the research involved can deepen understanding, as well as heighten appreciation of the materials acquired. Graeme Hanson, M.D., UCSF professor of psychiatry, also sees collecting as a mix of acquisitiveness and intellectual curiosity that's propelled by an urge for immortality, topped with a tinge of showing off.² As it stands, focus on a given category also affords the collector an opportunity to become expert with regard to their given interest.

So some individuals collect to elevate their social standing, while others collect as a form of investment and asset accumulation. The aggregation of particular types of objects, such as the possession of all coins or paintings in a specific series, can increase their value.

Most folks save objects of sentimental value, yet hoarders like Walter fail to distinguish between an article of sentiment and useless trash. According to their highly creative mindset, every object's possibilities are limitless, which means that everything is of value. Therefore, at some future date, a use for it may arise.

Finding and then possessing a Ming Dynasty vase, one that nobody else has, can be extremely gratifying. One-time president of the International Olympic Committee, the controversial Avery Brundage, happened to visit an exhibit of Chinese art at the Royal Academy in London back in 1936 and made the following comment: "We [he and his first wife] spent a week at the exhibition and I came away so enamored with Chinese art that I've been broke ever since."³ Using a systematic approach to collecting, Brundage eventually became a foremost authority on Asian Art.

At one time, our Dad's boss, Elliot Frankl, was renown for owning the world's largest private collection of Picassos. Apparently, for the likes of Mr. Frankl, the purpose of collecting meant surrounding oneself with objects of beauty. For others like Avery Brundage, what predominantly began as a quest for asset allocation, ended up involving careful consideration as to how he wanted to be seen by future generations. Brundage donated part of his vast collection to the city of San Francisco on the condition that they build a facility to house it.

At last count, Bruce had saved nearly 100,000 unread emails. Although he admittedly had no plans to ever attend to them, he also couldn't bear to press the delete button. For self-confessed digital hoarders, as hard drives get bigger and cloud storage gets cheaper, it's easy to carry around a lifetime of obscure digital debris. Many of these folks also hang onto inconsequential emails, or obsolete Word documents, or even selfies that they claim to dislike.

While technology has made us all into aggregators of information, Ingrid Schaffner, curator of Philadelphia's Institute of Contemporary Art remarks that, "Collecting is just another way of organizing thought."[4]

When I heard that a physician of Janice's acquaintance had a garage laden with medical journals, it occurred to me that *mental hoarding*, or the sequestering of information and ideas, might actually be *a thing*. Certainly, the Internet offers unlimited space where ideas and objects of desire are saved in abundance. Which brings me to Pinterest and how it relates to hoarding.

Type the word *Pinterest* on the laptop, hit enter, and one is immediately assaulted by myriad photos of crocheted doilies, favorite cookie recipes, along with limitless, head-spinning decorating ideas. The times I've ventured onto the site, I feel overwhelmed.

So, why the hype?

Basically, Pinterest serves as an place to save, organize and share images. Ardent fans claim that the social aspect offers a great way to discover and share things that one would dearly love to possess. Some actually attest that Pinterest affords them with a healthy outlet for their hoarding tendencies. As they clump together, or *pin*, objects that they admire, the urge to collect and curate is alleviated to the extent they needn't buy a thing.

"It's a great outlet for my need to possess, and a way to keep my ideas organized," says Jasmine, a big do-it-yourself advocate. "Plus, it redirects my desire to collect by allowing me to feel as if that thing I admire or covet is within easy reach."

"On the other hand," she admits, "surfing through [the site] eats up a lot of time and energy, and heightens my tendency to obsess. Sometimes, I feel overwhelmed, especially when unable to leave Pinterest alone."

It would appear that Pinterest users—by virtue of offering the option to aggregate vast numbers of items—display some hoarding characteristics, and that participation encourages hoarding-related behavior. That being said, hoarding, as clinically defined, isn't caused by this social photo sharing site.

When asked why they collect many retort, "because it's a blast." The more introspective admit that they do so simply because they have to. Then again, there are forms of collecting that stem from challenging life experiences. A fellow who'd been imprisoned in a Russian Gulag, for example, spent the remainder of his days amassing keys.

While the objects of desire may be symbolic, all are imbued with intrinsic value to the collector. Some individuals even admit that their passion for a particular doohickey is inexplicable.

Whether it's Barbie Dolls, desiccated butterflies, baseball cards, snow flurry paperweights, Beanie Babies, Wedgwood stoneware, seashells, or rare orchids smuggled out of a tropical jungle, many collect simply because everyone else does. In high school I had a penchant for psychedelic rock-and-roll posters; my sister collected silver and pewter spoons. Who knows why, but a pal of mine collected, then embedded dead insects in Elmer's Glue-All. Our mother was an aficionado of native California Indian artifacts, which we returned to the Ohlone tribe after her death. Jay Leno acquires sports cars; Oprah Winfrey and Bill Cosby share a fondness for austere Shaker furniture.

Initially, collecting was only pursued by the privileged. In part, such behaviors may have originally arisen in humans from a need to exert control, and then probably expanded as a result of curiosity about this world of ours. African headhunters kept the human skulls of their enemies that they'd killed in battle. Pharaoh Amenhotep III amassed blue enamels, while Philip II of Spain had a thing for holy relics.

Acquiring 7000 items in all, Philip of Spain's vast trove included ten corpses, as well as 144 human heads, 306 arms and legs, along with thousands of bones and body parts. Additionally, King Philip was attested to possess fragments of the "True Cross." (Given that numerous others claimed to possess pieces of it, entire forests must have been felled!)

Presumably, Christ was endowed with the standard number of limbs. Yet twenty-nine European locales lay claim to the holy nails that impaled him. On yet a more macabre note, a bitter rivalry ensued during the Middle Ages with—count 'em—eight individuals who allegedly possessed Jesus' *True Foreskin*!

Then there's the Russian Tsar Peter the Great who stockpiled assorted freakish oddities, including an exhibit of live human beings. As a self-dubbed surgeon, he also enjoyed personally excising and saving human teeth. As a result, many poor souls whose chompers he admired were forced to relinquish them. The Tsar *did*, however, transition his collection from private to public viewing and specifically invited his subjects to visit free of charge.

In the 1830s, while Spaniard Father Don Vincente served as monastery librarian, every one of the community's precious books went missing; the rascally priest also disappeared along with them. Shortly thereafter, one Don Vincente, dealer of rare books, appeared on the scene! Then, when a highly coveted book collection came to auction, he found himself bested.

In short order, the winning bidder was found dead, and a rash of murders swept the region. No small coincidence, all of the victims loved books.

Theft and murder aside, the demarcation between collecting as a hobby versus compulsive hoarding blurs when the neighbor's gnome collection overflows their yard onto the one adjacent and their unsightly junk mounds reduce property values. Or when Patty, whom we met earlier, rents a dozen storage units to house her book collection, and then cannot afford to pay for them.

The distinction between hoarding and collecting might compare to that of a social drinker as opposed to an alcoholic, or to a church-going bingo player in contrast to the lost-in-Las Vegas gambler. If collecting and the space the collection occupies doesn't interfere with one's life, and doesn't impinge on anyone else's existence, it's probably within an acceptable range. A big difference between the collector and hoarder is that the former appreciates what they've got and knows where everything is, whereas the latter hasn't any idea what they possess and cannot locate anything, but risks loss of it all in order to hang on to every scrap of it.

⌂⌂ ⌂

Exactly why an individual prefers one category of objects as opposed to another is a mystery. All surfaces of Sharon's home are strewn with collectible pigs: pink pigs, polka-dotted pigs, pigs in overalls, pigs doing jigs, pigs on bikes, pigs eating spare-ribs, and pigs simply being pigs.

"I haven't the foggiest idea why I'm so enamored, but I have this insatiable urge to possess every ceramic pig on the planet," muses Sharon, a social worker and single parent. "I guess I like them because they make me smile."

Given a life-long tendency to depression, Sharon attests to brief moments of satiety each time she acquires another pig. With regard to her attachment—her search, her longing, and the acquiring—she notes, "Collecting offers me a constant, ready-made friend. See...I'm single now and this activity fills the void. And, no, I don't find real pigs of interest at all."

Engaging in the ritual of the hunt helps soothe her uncertainty, and the thrill of acquisition helps discharge her chronic anxiety. So when life gets tough, Sharon shops.

Safe to say, pig collecting has become a familiar, well-worn groove for her. Over time, that groove's become a rather deep trench that's impossible for her to climb out of, for she frets that her penchant has or will take over her life. True, she holds down a job, cares for her children, grocery shops, and seems to manage okay. Yet her urge to own just one more pig has become—as per her own admission—insatiable.

Although all household surfaces are covered with kick-knacks, Sharon doesn't quite consider herself a hoarder. Aware of the need to keep purchases under control and within budget, coupled with the fact that her home is mostly functional and organized, at this point Sharon seems poised at that fine line between collecting and hoarding.

"Collections have an inherent tinge of mortality and decay, and exist in response to the "trauma of aloneness," notes Werner Muensterberger in his book, *Collecting: An Unruly Passion*.[5] Collecting can also signal a deep love for human enterprise, or a longing to understand, or the desire to celebrate or to chronicle our fragile existence. Indeed, collections help to create meaning in a world that so often overwhelms.

Muensterberger further likens collecting to the recurrent need to replenish oneself. Regardless of how often or how much one eats, he points out, one must repeatedly face hunger again. As if to satisfy an empty stomach, the collector finds it impossible to remain fulfilled. Another way to put it: collecting fills emptiness.[6]

Consciously or unconsciously, the roots of such passion can often be traced to one's formative years. Like the hoarder, some extreme collectors endured dire circumstances in childhood: they may have experienced war, parental suicide, divorce, illness, a physical handicap, starvation, or abuse. In such instances, acquiring temporarily mitigates these wounds and offers the promise of healing.

Newspaper tycoon William Randolph Hearst imported entire Gothic ceilings, as well as choir stalls, staircases, stained glass, and countless other European riches to fill his palatial estate in San Simeon, California. As with Hearst's penchant to amass, and Sharon's infatuation with ceramic pigs, such activities can be a source of comfort.

During a difficult interval, Janice took up shopping and buying to excess on eBay as an alternative to ingesting an antidepressant. Distracting herself with the search, she enjoyed the find, and then, as if a high-stakes gambler, placed aggressively competitive bids. With each win, while savoring the pleasure, she eagerly anticipated her package's arrival. But for each new item taken in, she rid herself of an old one.

Also for Janice and many others, the point of collecting seems to have to do with the fun of the pursuit. Yet accrual for many, including my sister, has little to do with usefulness or commercial value, but is about emotions.

Prominent and ordinary collectors, many regarded as eccentric or lonely, have an urge to collect that stems from a need for connection or as a substitute for love. Given the palliative impact imbued within a China-headed doll or a Lionel train set, some attest that these items are easier to bond with.

Rather than invest time and energy in untrustworthy humans, hoarders as well as collectors seek to approximate human surrogates. Such an affinity is common with animal hoarders in particular. Their preference for animals over human contact can stave off loneliness and even rage. Clearly, compilation of beloved paperweights or of a whole passel of cats can't possibly spurn one's affections!

Following her death, career nanny, Vivian Maier's employers found a tidily stored stash of photographic negatives amid a whole lot of other inexplicable odd items, which they then sold at auction. Luckily the buyer, grasping the significance of the cache of 100,000 photographs, made the film, *Finding Vivian Maier*. This film introduced Maier to the world and earned her a posthumous reputation as one of America's most accomplished street photographers.

With hints of a disturbingly dark side, questions have arisen as to whether this woman ever intended to develop those negatives for public consumption. Similar to a hoarder, perhaps she was merely compelled to take pictures and store them. And one wonders further: given her remote relationship with fellow beings, did her version of collecting possibly indicate the existence of an asocial personality, meaning did she share a stronger bond with her photographic negatives than she did with humans?

Since collecting can involve the search for the equivalent of love that went lacking during those formative years, some direct their longing onto religious or spiritual pursuits. Others assume caretaking roles, while a certain few harness that drive to claw their way to billionaire status. Then there are the average, straight-up collectors who amass in order to enhance or to restore their sense of self-worth.

British book and manuscript collector Sir Thomas Phillipps, whose life spanned 1792 to 1872, avidly pursued a single copy of every book in existence. At death, he'd acquired 50,000 tomes and 60,000 manuscripts. With a cache that included all known Mesopotamian cylinder seals—such seals, often intricate in design, were integral to daily life in Mesopotamia—Phillipps had the largest collection of manuscripts owned by a single person at that time. Additionally, he possessed countless documents, letters, and maps. Such abundance filled his home floor to ceiling, yet caused him to disregard the needs of his ailing wife and family to the extent that they lived in abject squalor.

It may help to know that Sir Thomas was the illegitimate son of a self-made merchant. Shortly after his birth, his mum, a lowly servant, got sent away, so he was raised by his schoolmaster. Possibly driven by loss and abandonment, incapable of establishing meaningful human attachment, he began the single-minded, self-centered obsession to collect books.

Safe to say, Sir Thomas Phillipps crossed over from collector to hoarder!

Conversely, rather than offer a means of coping with loneliness and isolation, collecting creates a plethora of opportunities to interact with kindred souls who share the same passion. Businesses and various organizations, along with special societies, as well as topic-specific publications, along with television programs such as *Antique Road Show, Comi-Con* and *Star Trek* conventions, and even Ebay, pander to our voracious desire to connect and to belong.

Collecting-related activities help us establish commonality and offer excellent opportunities to socialize. As an aside, the process of amassing and marketing nostalgia, allows fond memories, embedded within objects to evoke recollection of easier, simpler times.

Upon arrival at the home of my airline stewardess friend, Dinny, I behold a behemoth thirty-foot-long shipping container that fills her entire driveway. "What's with the trailer," I ask as we greet.

"Er, that's my closet," Dinny laughs, rolling her eyes. "When I travel, I've developed this nasty compulsion to shop and bring back clothes and gifts.— Want to see?"

When she swings the bay doors open, I behold an ocean of garments inside that are crammed to the ceiling. Price tags dangling, clothes still scrunched in Saks, Bloomingdale's, or Victoria's Secret shopping bags, fill the entire space.

"I'm really into clothes," she gushes. "As you see, I've never worn any of this. Some I plan to keep, but most of it I want to give away. I'm always worried that I won't have the perfect gift when needed, so I buy stuff duty-free when I travel. It's become a kind of joke, though; when I try to find something to give as a gift, I can't decide, so I end up keeping it all. This here's the result."

Dinny is a childhood pal; it's been a long time between visits, so we catch up over lunch. At some point, I excuse myself to use the loo. Unable to resist, I peek into her bedrooms; these, too, are filled with garments. Bedrooms aside, the rest of her home remains warmly attractive.

Onward we chat, catching up on each other's lives and gossiping about family. She fixes a divine Reuben sandwich—bread toasted to perfection, crunchy sauerkraut, thinly-sliced pastrami and Swiss cheese—I'm in heaven!

As we circle back to her garment stash, she resumes, "My family criticizes me for spending so much money on clothes. My brother once rented a Uhaul, and insisted we empty the place out, but I refused. He called me an obsessive hoarder, which I *so* am not! It's just that buying things gives me a nice high. Strangely, though, the mere thought of throwing or giving stuff away makes me pretty darn nervous."

From outward appearance, my friend seems reasonably content; she's happily married, has held down a job that she loves for twenty years, and has a ton of friends. Aside from the shipping container and those jam-packed bedrooms, she has a lovely, functioning home.

"I guess I'm what you call a compulsive shopper," she confesses. "There've been times when I've extended our credit beyond our means, which led to a whole lot of debt. Poor Don attributes my sprees to mania, as manic depression runs in my family. But I'm certainly not, not, not..." she wags a finger, "depressed!"

Although Dinny denies having droopy spirits, I see hints of it throughout our visit. Depression, coupled with poor impulse control, are behaviors prevalent among hoarders.

Depressed, or not, I'm pretty sure Dinny, bright, bubbly, always fun, my pal since forever, is precariously perched between the netherworld of hoarding and collecting.

Collecting, it seems, is hoarding's more sophisticated, socially acceptable cousin. Whether one collects in an overt legacy-making fashion, like art patron Avery Brundage, or acquires ceramic pigs that no one else will likely ever see, the highly individualized process helps to create certainty and order that's often lacking in our chaotic world.

CHAPTER 5

I'm Collecting as Fast as I can—OCD, with OCD Hoarding as a Sub-Set

---

"Avert the danger not arisen;"

—VEDIC PROVERB.

MILLIONAIRE BUSINESSMAN HOWARD HUGHES SPENT much of his final twenty years avoiding imagined dangers by engaging in a variety of mystifying, bizarre behaviors. Obsessed with germs and fearing contamination, he wrote out painstakingly detailed memos, directing his staff as to how to prepare his meals. To ingest food proved so onerous, that he ate only once daily, and often fasted for several days thereafter. Further, in keeping with his "backflow of germs theory," he once declined to send flowers to the funeral of a close friend who'd died of hepatitis-related complications for fear the hepatitis germ might "flow" back to him.

Beset with fears run amok, poor Howard Hughes was plagued with myriad obsessive-compulsive concerns regarding contamination. The American Psychiatric Association defines an Obsessive-Compulsive Disorder as a chronic anxiety disorder characterized by obsessive thoughts, along with compulsive behaviors that are excessive, time-consuming, and interfere with a person's ability to function. Howard Hughes had OCD and its attendant problems, big-time!

These obsessive thoughts repeatedly flood the mind, are persistent, irrational, intrusive, often disturbing, and are extremely tough get rid of. By engaging in their compulsive rituals, individuals with OCD seek to avoid unpleasant thoughts and situations.

OCD sufferers often exhibit a co-morbidity with other disorders that may include depression, eating and anxiety disorders, schizophrenia, dementia, and mental retardation. One study found the frequency of OCD in patients with multiple sclerosis to be 16.1%.[1]

Cursed with multiple OCD symptoms, Howard Hughes was also a hoarder. "He could not bear to part with anything that was his," reads a segment from Michael Drosnin's book, *Citizen Hughes*. "Not his dust, not his junk, not his hair, not his fingernails, not his sweat, not his urine, not his feces. His hair and beard went uncut for years; he stopped trimming his nails when he somehow "lost" his favorite clippers in the debris of his lair; he stored his urine in capped jars kept first in his Bel-Air garage and later in his Las Vegas bedroom; and he was so chronically constipated, so unable to dispose of his bodily wastes that he once spent twenty-six consecutive hours sitting on the toilet without results."[2]

Some hoarders are also obsessed with symmetry, while others have a compulsion to count. Additionally, many of them are plagued with tics—the twitchy, rather than insect kind—and also exhibit pathological grooming behaviors that include skin picking, nail biting, and trichotillomania, which involves the yanking out of hair. By-in-large, OCD sufferers who hoard tend to have more severe symptoms, along with other co-occurring disorders.[3]

While the anxiety-driven Howard Hughes feared contamination from germs and dirt, he also performed repetitive, ritualistic behaviors that involved endless counting and checking. Washing his hands and entire body to extreme, he also constantly cleansed his environment, as well. If those compulsions weren't challenging enough, he felt compelled to touch, spin, tap, rhyme, organize, and arrange, while repeatedly requesting reassurance.

Counter-intuitively, such behaviors stem from a striving for perfection. "Hoarders tend to be perfectionists," notes Kimberly Rae Miller, whose father hoards and her mother shops to excess, "that each item they collect is one critical part of an ideal world they are ever-creating for themselves."[4]

Compulsions show up as repeated pesky rituals that one must perform in an attempt to prevent or to assuage anxiety. Sub-categories include the following: *checkers* who must repeatedly reassure themselves that no harm awaits; *doubters and sinners* who fear they'll be punished if everything isn't just so; *counters and arrangers* who are obsessed with order, symmetry, and precision; and, like Howard Hughes, *washers and cleaners* who fear contamination, and well...they do as previously described.

Actress, Cameron Diaz is a washer and a cleaner who only opens doors with her elbows, as she refuses to touch germ-laden doorknobs with her bare hands. Driven by a fear of germs, as previously mentioned, these germophobes repeatedly scrub themselves.

While the act of washing provides temporary relief from anxiety, it doesn't eradicate one's unreasonable fear of germs. As a result, the individual keeps right on washing, thereby creating a vicious, unrelenting cycle.

Fear of germs doesn't automatically mean one has OCD. Most who engage in good hygiene practices aren't too keen on germs either, and it's good practice for us all to wash up at intervals throughout the day. However, normal hygienic practice turns into OCD when the urge to wash takes over to disrupt everything.

Shelly, a housewife, checks the lights and locks a hundred times over. Spending so much time doing so, she misses appointments and rarely leaves home. James must arrange, then rearrange, his underwear and sock drawers, ad nauseam.

Compulsions can take the form of *meticulous grooming rituals*. As Evan combs his hair, he makes certain each strand lies precisely so. Should a single hair slip from place, he must begin the entire process over again. Compulsions may also take the form of mental gymnastics. As a combination of a *doubter, sinner,* and a *checker*; during her drive to work, Maude must pass over every bridge in town. This diversion tacks on an extra hour to what would otherwise be a ten-minute trek, yet she fears an apocalyptic outcome should she skip any part of the specific sequence.

Similarly, Missy feels obliged to crack each knuckle of every toe and finger as she simultaneously recites the Lord's Prayer. She must perform this routine to perfection before permitting herself to drift off to sleep. There are others who are compelled to continually whisper complex incantations to prevent whatever horrid outcome they wish to avoid. Marvin suspects someone will be murdered if he departs from home without donning his favorite tie. Although able to laugh at himself, he wears the tie while mowing the lawn for fear of hazarding an adverse outcome.

While compulsive gamblers and shoppers, as well as those with drug or alcohol abuse issues derive a modicum of pleasure from their habits, OCD compulsives find no pleasure or enjoy no benefit from their actions. On the contrary, their activities exhaust, deplete and limit life, and merely serve as joyless attempts to reduce anxiety or to stave off dreaded imaginings.

Steve, a business executive, frets that the coffee at work is contaminated, and insists that he be the sole person to make it. As a result, he arrives at the office several hours early to prepare the quintessential cup. Perpetually dissatisfied with the results, he tosses out pot after pot, as he then tries to perfect it over again. Whereas the rest of us would simply swear off coffee, the ever-determined Steve is stuck in an endless loop.

Sydney, a middle-aged computer operator, feels responsible for the safety of others. As a result, he lives in terror, lest he run over a pedestrian while driving his car. Incapable of heading directly to work, he repeatedly returns to sites along his route to check for injured persons and dead bodies. Additionally, he must cross back and forth between the many overpasses that dot his journey to inspect, then recheck, girders and beams for structural safety. Understandably given to chronic tardiness, he's not exactly endeared to his boss.

Some with OCD diverge from the typical hoarder insofar as those with straight-up OCD know that their urges are irrational, excessive, and a waste of time, yet are unable to cease acting upon them. Often, they're so mortified that they go to great lengths to hide their symptoms. This secrecy prevents them from seeking professional help that might make a vast difference. Commonly, when they *do* reach out, rather than divulge the true nature of their problem they complain of depression or anxiety.

Not to be confused with OCD, Obsessive Compulsive Personality Disorder (OCPD) is characterized by a preoccupation with orderliness, perfectionism, and interpersonal control, at the expense of flexibility, openness, and efficiency. For example, anger may be expressed as righteous indignation over a seemingly minor matter.

People with OCPD also tend to be overly concerned with their relative status within hierarchical relationships. Deferential to an extreme in the face of authority, they're conversely resistant and dismissive of individuals they disdain. Their expressions of affection come off as stilted and highly controlled and their relationships tend to be formal and serious.

According to Lorrin Koran, M.D., of Stanford University Medical Center who studied the impact of OCD on the quality of life experienced by patients and their families, 90% of the hoarders in the cohort *did* recognize their actions to be irrational, and made repeated promises to clean up, but never did so. Most of them saw no reason to seek treatment, and their denial, resistance, as well as their tendency to minimize the impact of problem worsened over time. Furthermore, the OCD hoarders in the study were less likely to have insight regarding their behaviors than participants who manifest other types of OCD.[5]

At the onset of their disorder, OCD hoarders may actually know their obsessions and actions to be irrational, yet after years of entrenchment, they lose discernment as to appropriate behaviors, and begin to defend their actions as essential. This happens because obsessive-compulsive behaviors tend to be self-reinforcing, meaning the more frequently a behavior is performed, the more deeply ingrained it becomes. Repetition causes aberrant acts to become rigidly affixed, which makes them tough to eradicate.

Hoarding has been defined and described in various ways in relation to OCD: some deem it a symptom of OCD, others see it as a variant of OCD, while still others view it as a manifestation of OCD. Remember Norman, that sweet-pie hoarder? He's beset with OCD hoarding.

At any rate, as previously noted, OCD hoarders tend to exhibit more severe symptoms and have a higher degree of functional impairment than their OCD counterparts who do not hoard.

There can be other reasons one might display hoarding symptoms that aren't precisely what's defined as compulsive hoarding. An individual may be too depressed to put things away or to organize and clean up their space, yet their actions may look like hoarding. One may also be in the throes of another psychiatric problem such as a psychosis that results in the aggregation of too many things. Dementia or Prader-Willi Syndrome—a genetic disorder that is due to the loss of function of specific genes—can also involve hoarding. One might also hoard as an aspect of yet another OCD compulsion. For instance, a person who fears contamination may hang on to library books, stemming from concern that they've contaminated them and, as a result can't bring them back. This action doesn't necessarily define them as being a hoarder.

⌂⌂ ⌂

Often hoarding manifests in several members of the same family. That an individual raised by a hoarder grows up and displays similar hoarding behaviors makes me wonder if the behavior is learned or genetic, so we'll take a look at this shortly.

OCD hoarding affects about 2.2 million American adults, with one-third of adult hoarders attesting to the early onset of their behaviors, where their symptoms manifest in childhood or during their teen years.[6] There's also a high probability that the hoarder has a family member or two who manifests other OCD symptoms. Overall, hoarding is seen as a progressive journey. Behaviors tend to gradually emerge, increasing in severity over time, with flare-ups during stress-filled intervals.

Beginning in childhood with the accumulation of specific items, hoarding morphs into the somewhat innocuous purchase of, or the saving of extra food and household supplies, till eventually the activity blossoms into collecting, full-time.[7] Although symptoms *do* wax and wane, OCD tends to be chronic and progressive, with impairment ranging from mild to out-of-control. As a rule, if left untreated the compulsions don't disappear on their own.

Yet, oddly, rare individuals *do* simply outgrow their OCD disorder. Colorful radio personality, Howard Stern claims to have exerted his intention and will to make his compulsive behaviors disappear, (He declines to identify the precise nature of his OCD challenge.) but he's a rarity.

Some with OCD sustain successful careers, but when symptoms overwhelm, it's incredibly tough for them to hold down a job. Given the enormous time and energy spent performing those exhaustive obsessive-compulsive rituals, coupled with attempts to hide the problem, the sufferer may become so thoroughly diverted that they are unable to sustain employment, or maintain a household, or keep up with relationships, let alone relate to family.

○○ ○

Now and then, I fumble about in my backpack for keys or go check the door to make certain it's locked, but I only admit to checking once to satisfy my doubt. There's my acquaintance Stuart, however, who leaves the house, wonders if the door is bolted, and must go back to check:

Yes, the door's definitely locked.

Into his car he climbs, starts the engine, then wonders all over again: *How's that door doing, is it really secure?*

So out he clambers, goes back and checks, just to be certain.

Whew, all's fine!

Returned to the car, all buckled up, off he drives. Yet, doubt rears up again.

Is that door really latched? Not really sure. Better go back and check to be safe. Around the block he goes, exits the car, and twists the door knob. *Yup, it's locked!*

Back in the car, off he drives. Yet he still continues to fret, for his brain is jammed in an exhaustingly futile, never-ending loop.

OCD is known as a "disease of doubt." Unable to distinguish between what's possible, what's probable, and what's unlikely to occur, these doubters undergo seismic levels of pathological uncertainty that define and rule their lives.

Like Howard Hughes, Leticia, who is a hoarder, worries about germs so she scrubs her hands till they're chapped, raw, and bloody. Each time the phone rings, she must wash up to perfection before it's safe to lift the receiver, and constantly misses calls. Heaven forbid she touch an object without donning gloves, for then she must scrub all over again. "It's an insanely stupid waste of time and energy," she laments, "yet, I cannot stop."

When James organized all plaids in a fabric store, the clerk asked him to cease, but he was unable to comply. Previously banned from the local supermarket, he couldn't refrain from sorting candies according to color.

Personally, I can relate, for I find it intolerable to see off-kilter picture frames hanging on walls. And when I notice kindred objects that are improperly spaced, I'm compelled to nudge them into place.

Ritualized behavior is common among children; often it arises as a result of superstition. Many of us as youngsters avoided stepping on cracks, or annoyingly ate only red foods, or checked beneath the bed for monsters. As a child, I habitually counted in sequences of 7, 13, and 33 to relax. My sister's nightly ritual involved recitation of an extensive series of prayers. Should she drift off and forget her place, she had to repeat entire the process over again. Thankfully, we outgrew such silliness, whereas those hard-hit compulsives do not.

Tennis star and winner of the Australian Open men's championship, Rafael Nadal, may or may not be an obsessive compulsive, yet several of his behaviors suggest that he is. Seemingly seeking to mitigate stress and to control anxiety, Nadal routinely performs what is termed his "square walk," then he carefully lines up his water bottles in a row, with all labels facing a prescribed direction. Lastly, he runs his thumb and finger down his nose before each shot played. Nadal may merely be superstitious and possibly executes these routines as a manifestation of the control that athletes commonly seek, and clearly, his behaviors don't pose a problem to his game. Yet it appears to many that he has OCD.

Overall, the rituals of persons with OCD differ markedly from folks who are merely superstitious, as the latter associates certain objects, actions, and events with bad or good fortune, and then tries to avoid them or to immunize themselves with them. Yet OCD sufferers engage in rituals that far surpass ordinary superstitious habits and beliefs. These folks know with frightening, highly-charged certainty that if they fail to act something terrible will befall them or cause harm to another. It's not uncommon for a compulsive individual to circle round the block time and again, until they feel sufficiently safe and settled to enter their house or another building while they are out and about.

Freud proffered the observation: "Compulsive disorders are a 'private religion' and religious rites are a collective compulsion." Dr. Robert Frost, in his 1993 study, revisits Freud's theory to find that hoarders, acting on the urge to control their surroundings, seek to ward off disaster.[8]

Speaking of religion, the Catholic who goes to confession to cleanse and remove sins is assigned by the priest to recite twelve Hail-Marys and five Our Fathers, which raises the question: does this repetition—the so-called washing away and warding off—bear any semblance to the behavior of a compulsive?

△△ △

In addition to OCD hoarding, several other OCD subsets exist. Some individuals, like Sydney, experience intrusive, unwanted, distressing concern, lest they cause or have already caused *harm*. This fear pivots around the belief that one must be in control at all times in order to keep from committing a violent or fatal act. Such thoughts tend to be ego-dystonic, meaning they're inconsistent with the individual's values, beliefs, and sense of self.

Religious-based intrusive thoughts are another form of OCD, wherein one fixates on morality and religious practices. The term *scrupulosity* applies to these folks and they tend to fear committing a sin so heinous that God will never forgive them, which then results in eternal damnation. Fearing such condemnation, an individual may exert extraordinary effort, for example, to return a measly ten cents when they've been undercharged.

Another OCD offshoot involves focus on obsessive *health concerns*. Regardless of how many medical tests this person undergoes, and despite the fact that all the tests are spotlessly normal, he or she is convinced that they're in the throes of a terrible illness. This isn't your garden variety hypochondriac who is beset with somatic delusions and goes overboard with anxious paroxysms pertaining to being or getting sick. These OCD sufferers know with absolute certainty, despite all evidence to the contrary, that they're teetering on the brink of death—every moment of their lives revolve around this.

Maxine, who is perfectly healthy, believes her death is imminent if she neglects to follow her compulsion to collect. Fear of failure in this regard causes her extreme anxiety and panic. Despite the fact that she's a rational, highly intelligent woman, and even comments about the oddity of her behaviors, she repeatedly apologizes that she cannot curtail her actions. So, daily at the crack of dawn, Maxine parks her station wagon outside a nearby thrift store to eagerly await its opening.

Hours pass until the doors swing open, and then Maxine scurries inside. As if she's a participant in that old televised show *Supermarket Sweep,* she makes a mad dash, tossing garments, furniture, household items, and books—especially books—into her shopping cart. When the cart is filled, she pays up, shoves the stuff into her car, and drives home, where she chucks her newfound booty into her already crammed residence or tosses it in her yard.

Task finished, she returns to the store to fill a cart again.

Following up on a complaint about her behavior, my co-author, Janice drives to a pristine, wealthy seaside neighborhood and pulls up in front of Maxine's abode. Impossible to miss the teetering henges of junk in the yard, as one might imagine, the odd sight of the jumble has the neighbors perpetually miffed.

Inherently a civil bunch, they initially attempted an amicable resolution. After enduring subsequent years of the unsightly mess, however, along with her yard's adverse impact on their property values, they complained to the County.

So up to the door Janice goes in response to their behest, knocks, introduces herself, and explains the concerns.

Albeit reluctantly, Maxine permits a tour. In the backyard the partially drained swimming pool contains a profusion of rubbish and the stench that wafts from it is unbearable. Both of her side yards are also jammed with junk, making them impossible to traverse.

With no spare room inside to function, Maxine sleeps upright in a chair, showers at the homeless shelter, and dines at a nearby soup kitchen. Despite her unsafe, crowded environs, as well as the challenges she faces due to her actions, she fears something awful will happen should she throw anything away.

As a result, Maxine collects all day, every day, and has no other life. When thrift stores are closed, she frequents yard sales. As with many others, the shopping, the finding, the holding, the having, reduces distress to give her mere fleeting seconds of comfort.

Despite several previous assists from her children to clear the mess, the trash swiftly regrows. So they now refuse to lend a hand.

Each subsequent time government officials descend, she must hire help to clean up. Maxine now lives in terror lest she be cited, yet again, and continually worries that her home might be condemned.

In a former life, Maxine was a professor of philosophy, led a grand social circle, held parties, had a doting husband, and raised two charming daughters. As the envy of friends, her posh lifestyle and elegantly appointed home offered an existence that many would swoon over.

On the face of it, Maxine's daily activities seem absurdly self-destructive, but as Darwinian theorists suggest, these OCD symptoms seem to represent misplaced, survival-related strategies that stem from primitive behaviors. There was a time when our early antecedents relied on their thoughts and fears to protect from very real environmental dangers. The attentive, hyper-vigilant, cautious individual who carefully checked, organized, and ordered their environment survived, whereas, the casual, trusting, slothful one did not.

Maxine, like so many impacted by OCD, endures seismic, overwhelming urges that compel her to react to non-existent dangers. Although the underlying mechanisms or hoarding are not fully understood, it's posited that these imagined dangers, hard-wired into the nervous system, arise due to dysfunction or damage to certain brain centers.

Evidence further suggests that fear extinction, as well as behavioral inhibition, may be impaired for those with OCD. Modern day OCD compulsions are thought to be fragments of once purposeful activities that now arise inappropriately due to the dysfunction of the brain's cortico-striato-thalamo-cortical circuitry.

In rudimentary terms, this circuitry drives and controls numerous body functions. Essentially, the thalamus receives sensory information from the external world and relays it to the brain's prefrontal cortex. The prefrontal cortex then processes this influx to make complex decisions as to how the individual should respond. While sensory information from the thalamus is crucial, too much activity can overwhelm the prefrontal cortex, thereby inhibiting activities of the thalamus in order to prevent sensory overload.

Mice who have had these same brain synapses surgically impeded tend to exhibit anxiety and also execute compulsive grooming behaviors. Parenthetically, both these behaviors are alleviated when antidepressants known as selective serotonin re-uptake inhibitors (SSRI) are administered.[9]

Of parallel curious note, autoimmune disorders arise when the body's immune system mistakenly attacks and destroys healthy body tissue. This hyper-immunization occurs in response to the presence of a specific antigen which triggers the body to create more antibodies than normal. As a result, the immune system goes haywire and cannot shut down. Similar to autoimmune diseases, OCD might be likened to a mental autoimmune system where those once essential primal protective reactions of anxiety, disgust, and fear now trigger obsessions and compulsions that exceed their usefulness and turn destructive.

While OCD and post-traumatic stress disorder (PTSD) differ with regard to key aspects—for one, PTSD does not manifest compulsive rituals—similarities *do* exist between them. With PTSD, the individual relives traumatic experiences through vivid, excruciating nightmares and flashbacks. As a result, sleep and stability can be elusive to the extent that sufferer feels detached and has difficulty performing everyday functions. Similar to PTSD, the obsessive thoughts of OCD can surge during, or subsequent to, traumatic or life-threatening situations.

Related to this, data shows that women undergo a significant increase in OCD behaviors during pregnancy and childbirth. As one might expect, these behaviors also surge following the death of a loved one, and also heighten subsequent to other times of loss. Yet again, from an evolutionary perspective, both PTSD and OCD seem to be pathological extensions of adaptive responses that once facilitated survival or risk reduction, but have now run amok.[10]

△△ △

Often, OCD is misdiagnosed as autism, a disorder characterized by problems with language or communication, as well as impaired social interaction, and may include repetitive behaviors and rigidity. OCD can also be mistaken for a developmental disorder or as Tourette Syndrome (TS).

Tourette's is a neurological debility typified by repetitive, involuntary movements and also by vocalizations, called tics. Such tics may be classified as *simple* or *complex*. *Simple* motor tics manifest as sudden, brief, and repetitive actions that can include eye blinking, grimacing, shrugging, sniffing, throat clearing, and sometimes barking.

One of the worst variations is know as coprolalia; the involuntary and repetitive blurting of obscenities. As a child growing up, I was terrified by an older boy, Michael, who often blurted out a stream of scary, naughty invective. Yet, as a soloist for our church choir, the purity of his voice came out as sheer, harmonic bliss.

Complex tics show up in the performance of an intricate series of coordinated movements produced by a number of muscle groups or through vocalizations. Examples of complex motor tics include touching objects or other people, jumping up and down, spinning around, or imitating someone's actions (echopraxia). Tics may also display as inappropriate gestures or behaviors (copropraxia), and vocal tics involve repeating a phrase over and over, whether it's something one has just heard (echolalia) or one's own recent words (palilalia).

A young man of my acquaintance with Tourette's exclusively produced guttural throat noises for months on end, but then abruptly took up neck contortions, along with eye blinks for several ensuing months. When his birthday came round, a surprise party was given and the crowd shouted, "Happy Birthday!" Taken aback, he ceased to twitch and repeatedly blurted, "Happy Birthday" to his well-wishers.

Those beset with such tics often seek to make them seem purposeful. I have a relative who skillfully disguises her compulsive head bobs and shoulder twitches as smooth dance moves. Most dramatic and disabling are tics that cause harm; punching oneself in the face, for instance.

Tics tend to worsen with excitement or anxiety. As one might expect, physical or emotional stress may activate, trigger, or heighten them. While tics can persist during sleep, their frequency and vigor is significantly diminished. Once thought to be rare, Tourette's is rather commonplace. If one tunes into the neurobehavioral manifestations of Tourette's, with all its variations, notes neurologist Oliver Sacks, the disorder is easy to spot.

My family comprises a veritable solar system of tics—some diagnosed, others not—and is replete with throat clearers, neck rotators, finger sniffers, and groaners. Janice admits to being an avid cheek muncher, who habitually savages the innards of her mouth. Our deceased Mom was a champion sniffer.

As if tics aren't enough, many with TS suffer additional neurobehavioral challenges. Problems with reading, writing, and arithmetic are common. Understandably, many sufferers also report depression, anxiety, and difficulties with general function.

Often of even greater impairment than the tics, however, are problems with inattention, hyperactivity, and poor impulse control. Should one posses these challenges, the diagnosis of Attention Deficit Hyperactivity Disorder (ADHD) may be added to their resume.

According to a 2009 study at John Hopkins, kindred genes tie Tourette's with OCD and ADHD, as well, which suggests that these disorders share common pathology. With Tourette's, abnormalities have also been identified in certain brain regions, specifically the circuit that connects the basal ganglia.

The brain's frontal lobes, as well as the cerebral cortex, and the neurotransmitters, dopamine, serotonin, and nor-epinephrine—which are responsible for communication among nerve cells—seem to be improperly wired.[11]

Given that several obsessive-compulsive variations exist, I began to wonder why one compulsive behavior arises over another, what switches it on, and what causes it to wax and wane over time. For instance, how does a hand washer morph into a checker and then later blossom into a full-fledged hoarder?

While emotional factors as well as family circumstances may prompt one obsession or compulsion to arise as opposed to another, there's no known biological reason as to why one person hoards and someone else is cursed to wash and to check.

⌂⌂ ⌂

With no definitive answers in hand, we return to Norman, the sweet man who adores McDonald's Happy Meal boxes, to see if we can unearth a bit of clarity. Over the years, Janice received calls from landlords to complain about his extreme trash accumulation. Each place he lived—flophouses, hotels, apartments—within days of arrival, the space filled up to burgeon with his salvaged treasure of choice: those cardboard containers.

"First time we met," Janice recounts, "he beamed, thrust out his hand, and said, 'I suppose you're here to chide me about my, er—little problem.' Round-faced, and cherubic, I found it impossible not to fall for this sweet-natured eighty year old guy."

As Janice explains the reason for her visit—to stave off his eviction—Norman folds his arms over his ample belly to interject: "When I was a boy, my daddy kept our house neat as a pin. If anything fell out of place—anything—if a spoon was imperfectly aligned, or if shoes weren't buffed to perfection and neatly organized, we got beaten. So nowadays, I thoroughly enjoy my messes." Face lit up, he shoots a wicked grin. "I guess you could say that I'm getting even."

"Sounds like a serious case of revenge clutter," Janice chimes, coining a new term.

"Wow, I like it!" Reaching out, Norman gives her a congratulatory tap.

⌂⌂ ⌂

Commonly, as we know, hoarders ascribe their hoarding urges to a critical, unloving parent, noting that buying or saving stuff offers a modicum of nurturing that they lacked when young. Since Freud's era, therapists sought to explain how childhood trauma can lead to adult dysfunction, so this concept works well in Norman's case.

Given that OCD tends to run in families, Norman's dad was probably an obsessive-compulsive. Growing up with such a rigid, dominating, perfectionist parent can later manifest as a compulsion to exert control.

As Norman continues, he's disarmingly forthcoming. "As a youngster, I carted home rocks by the thousands. I don't rightly know why I chose rocks. I guess because they didn't cost. With an itch to to possess, I gathered them up, brought them home, and left them piled in the yard. I never did anything with them, but always knew when my sister took one, which she sometimes did just to rile me."

As a pre-teen, Norman acquired a complex array of tics. As he passed through certain doorways, he was overtaken by a compulsion to tap the door frame, and then had to sequentially touch specific body parts, time and again. At intervals throughout the day, he also had to pause to systematically sniff each finger. "It got so bad, I stopped going to school in fifth grade."

Two years into his compulsive behaviors, the rituals mysteriously evaporated. By then, however, his compulsion to collect had metastasized into full-blown hoarding.

When grown, Norman's urge to bring home trash grew so complex, so time-consuming, that he lost one form of employment after another. His favorite job of postal clerk spelt disaster, as he managed to abscond with bags full of advertising mailers. It's no light matter to steal mail from the government, but he initially got off with merely a reprimand. Compelled to keep at it, eventually, he was fired. Out of work, he was then able to devote himself to hoarding, full-time.

At some point, at his wife's behest, he saw a psychiatrist who took note of his unresolved parental issues. "That part was a no-brainer," he announces to Janice, "and I certainly didn't need to pay someone to tell me what I already knew!"

Under duress from his wife he kept attending therapy, however, which helped him cope with depression. Yet not surprisingly, during all those years of counseling, he never managed to broach the topic of hoarding with the therapist. "Why would I want to stop," he blusters, "when collecting is my life!"

"There were times my wife would make me move things so she could open the refrigerator to prepare a meal," he recalls. "Before going to sleep at night, she also made me shove accumulated piles off the bed. Bad as it got, strange as it may seem, she and I never actually discussed my problem. Oh, she sighed, sulked and frowned a whole lot, but no...we never did talk about it. Eventually, after twenty-five years together, she'd had enough and left."

Home lost to foreclosure, Norman then got evicted from a series of apartments, and later from hotel rooms and flophouses; that's when Janice came into the picture.

"At one point, I paid rent on eight storage units, spending about $850 a month for them. Then, unable to keep up payments, I lost everything." Norman shakes his head, regretfully. "There was a whole lot of valuable stuff in there."

"These days, I get lonely and miss my daughter and wife, and wish I could be more organized and control my urges. But, I really *do* like being surrounded by all this."—he waves an arm to indicate his hotel room full of rubble. "When I'm here, I feel safe.

"See this box,"—he holds a Big-Mac Happy Meal carton aloft,—"I have no idea why, but having it makes me feel real good, so I can't toss it. It's just that simple."

Norman spends days pushing as many as five shopping carts, tethered together as he combs the streets to dumpster-dive and rummage through alleys in search of trash and treasure. Presently under the gun, he promises the hotel manager that he'll clear his room, but merely procrastinates.

When eviction day arrives, Janice shows up, armed with plastic bags and boxes, ready to toss out everything.

Norman opens the door to her knock to announce, "I don't feel so good."

Indeed, his nail beds are blue-tinged, he's short of breath, and his ankles are puffy, but when Janice offers a trip to the doctor, he declines.

Magazines, books, clothing, but mostly cardboard McDonald's boxes are piled high on the bed, making it impossible for him to lie down, so Janice suggests, "How about I take these out to the trash? It'll make space for you to put up your feet."

"No!" he rasps, turned frantic. "Sorry, but I need them."

With homelessness looming, Janice coaxes and cajoles.

Still, Norman refuses to part with anything.

"It's okay," he assures, "if they throw me out, I'll sleep in the park. Besides, I can go without food a day or two. See..."—he indicates his protruding belly—"I can certainly afford to live off my fat. It's the end of the month, so my check will come soon, and then I'll find another hotel.

"Also, if I get hungry, I know a few restaurants where I can go through their trash. Naturally, McDonald's is my favorite."

Janice groans, trying to reason. "If you don't clear this place, you'll be evicted and will lose this stuff anyway."

Eyes shut, Norman shakes his head.

Nothing goes into the trash, so Norman, alone and in failing health, is out on the street.

CHAPTER 6

Hoarding Cats and Dogs— Loving Animals to Death

"Animal hoarding was a dirty secret until hoarders appeared on our TV screens and showed how they are compelled to collect so many dogs, cats or parrots, and that they end up in cages, no bigger than their bodies. For life."

—INGRID NEWKIRK.

HORRID STENCH NOTWITHSTANDING, PASSERSBY GREW alarmed at the sight of a herd of goats confined in a crowded pen along the north coast of Santa Cruz, California. When the Humane Society arrived to investigate, they found over three hundred goats wallowing in a swamp of mud, urine, and feces. The animals were so badly caked with muck, they could barely hoof about. In terrible condition, clumps of hair had fallen out, leaving raw patches of flesh, and most of the goats had respiratory infections. With no access to clean water, what little liquid there was had turned fetid and stagnant, and swarmed with mosquito larvae.

Some of the goats' horns had been improperly removed, causing them to re-grow, doubled back upon themselves. In one poor billy's case, a horn had punctured its skull. Many of their untrimmed hooves curled up to cripple them. When their owner was questioned about their predicament, he huffed, "They can still walk, can't they?"

The Humane Society removed the goats and charged the landowners with cruelty. (Ironically, these creeps were renowned on the dairy circuit for their prize-winning animals.) Steadfastly adamant, they denied neglect, complaining that the Humane Society merely sought publicity for the sake of donations, and further protested that the goats were worse off under the organization's care.[1]

Unlike the animal hoarder, most animal rescue organizations and animal sanctuaries put the needs of their animals foremost. They recognize when they cannot provide good care, and when at capacity, they increase caretaking staff, stop intake of new animals, and improve or add more living space.

While hoarding goats is unusual, animals of varied species—horses, dogs, even fish and birds—are known to be hoarded. Yet cats seem to be the hoarder's animal of choice: they're compact, adapt to life indoors, and are easily hidden, which makes it tough for outsiders to discern how many of them reside within a home or even a vehicle.

Whereas most fanatic cat ladies try to hide their critter collection from the rest of the world, Cynthia Allen loaded her legion of felines into a van to take her cats on the road. When she arrived in Ontario, Oregon, animal rescue workers found that she'd crammed her 68 cats into her van.

"It was just a swirling mass of cats around your feet," notes Elizabeth Lyon of the Feral Cats Project. "Every step I took down that center aisle, I had to wiggle my foot in so I didn't step on somebody."

With only three litter boxes to serve the feline horde, the stench was reportedly "horrifying." Five dead cats were found, and many among the living were very emaciated. Some of them had lost an eye to infection; several had lost both eyes. One small male required emergency surgery to treat an eyeball that swelled out of its socket.[2]

Due to the bizarre nature of such incidents and the sheer numbers of animals involved, these occurrences often draw sensational media attention. While it may seem unfathomable, most of those who hoard animals believe themselves to be imbued with uniquely high levels of empathy with regard to their pets. Further, they firmly believe, despite all evidence to the contrary, that they provide outstanding care. In truth, they *are* devoted, but they also lack insight as to the consequences of their animals' impoverished living conditions.

Every community has its own precious cat lady—an eccentric, elderly soul whose life mission is to give refuge to dozens of stray felines. Despite good intentions, animal welfare groups often find these individuals unable to provide or to afford medical care, and that they don't spay or neuter them.

⌂⌂ ⌂

The Anxiety and Depression Association of America reports that 66% of animal hoarders are female; half of them live alone, and 46% are 60 years or older. Women tend to prefer cats, while men have a predilection for dogs. The median number of animals collected in a given hoarder's household is cited as thirty-nine, but several situations studied include over a hundred animals. In 80% of these cases, the animals were malnourished, ill, injured, or dead.[3]

According to a study at the Tufts University Center for Animals and Public Policy, approximately 200 to 700 instances of animal hoarding occur annually in the United States, while the American Society for Prevention of Cruelty to Animals (ASPCA) estimates that there are 900 to 2000 new cases every year, with over a quarter of a million animals involved.

Sadly, due to the covert nature of hoarding, coupled with a lack of reporting until a crisis arises, many instances of animal hoarding go unnoticed. As with other forms of hoarding, animal hoarding may be dismissed as merely a poor lifestyle choice, when really the issue is more complex.

Animal hoarding researcher Gary Patronek defines pathological animal hoarding as the accumulation of a large number of animals, coupled with the hoarder's failure to provide adequate nutrition, sanitation, and medical care for them. Animal hoarders are unaware of the over-crowded and unsanitary environment they've foisted upon their unfortunate pets. Even worse, they are often dismissive regarding their animals' deteriorating health.

Those who hoard animals justify their actions by asserting that no one else is capable of caring for their animals—or any animal—to the extent that they can. One hoarder of my acquaintance yells at passersby as they walk leashed dogs, insisting that the animals should be permitted to run free. Yet the animals in her care breed, overpopulate, and suffer from horrendous living conditions.

Added to the aforementioned behaviors, animal collectors fail to grasp the negative impact that the unhealthy conditions have on their own well-being and on that of their neighbors. Specifically, the inhalation of noxious levels of ammonia contained in animal urine is dangerous for human or for other live creature. Additionally, living in close proximity to animals who may be carriers of zoonotic disease—be it a virus, parasite, fungus, or bacteria—makes it highly plausible for a lethal illness to be passed from animal to human by way of feces. According to the Centers for Disease Control, six out of every ten infectious diseases found in humans is spread by animals.

In an attempt to understand why and how animal lovers devolve into animal abusers, Gail Steketee, social work professor at Boston University, performed a pilot study involving animal hoarders, which included individuals who possessed as many as 100 critters. "A fairly common thread," she notes, "in the cases we've looked at, is of people hoping to save animals. Somewhere along the line, they lose control. Then there are those who like animals a lot and do nothing as they breed out of control, and it overwhelms their abilities to care for the animals."

The New York Humane Society offers up a list of traits common to animal hoarders, which reads as follows: they neglect their personal physical and environmental conditions, tend to feel persecuted, attempt to justify their animal hoarding actions, attract others to help them continue their addictive behaviors, and have a knack for garnering sympathy.

The Hoarding of Animals Research Consortium, founded in 1997, performs ongoing investigation and also problem solves with regard to this matter. Devoted to human and animal welfare, their website shares the latest research information, as well as case studies, and legal updates.[4]

⌂⌂ ⌂

Pets have commonly played a significant role in the animal hoarder's childhood, which as previously noted, is often characterized as chaotic and unstable. As a result, these folks abandon trust in humankind, shunning human relations in favor of pets. Lacking human companionship, their creatures become central to their lives.

These people tend to anthropomorphize their animals, treat them as surrogate children, and allow them to run roughshod. Defecating and urinating wherever they please, these creatures climb about on counters where food is prepared, share the collector's bed, and even dine with them. As rapport grows, the hoarder over-identifies with their pets and experiences unconditional acceptance and love. Often, they also undergo profound grief when one of them dies.

Despite these strong emotions, once the critter is acquired, proper care and maintenance go by the wayside. Few animal hoarders actively abuse or intend to harm their pets, yet they generally cast a blind eye, refusing to provide medical care, or are incapable of safely managing them. Remarkably, some cannot even acknowledge when one of them is dead.

Adele, an elderly cat hoarder, argues, "Even if the animals die in my home, they're better off with me than at some scary, impersonal animal shelter. At the shelter, they just kill them."

Adele, it seems, confuses preservation of life at all costs with reverence for life.

As Pied Piper to many felines, Doris walks the railroad tracks, gathering up strays to bring home. With no idea how many of them reside inside or outside her house, she cannot afford to feed the entire horde, and since she refuses to spay them, their numbers rapidly multiply. For this and several other reasons, the neighbors complain to the authorities. So the County is tasked with reducing and controlling Doris' burgeoning cat population, which is a matter that she fiercely resists.

"I care for these cats," Doris announces as she first meets Janice, "because no one else will."

"Are you aware," Janice carefully inquires, "that there's a dead kitten lying in the grass near the driveway?"

"That kitty's not dead," Doris stoutly huffs as she goes to examine it. "It's resting."

Gently, Janice presses, "I'm pretty sure it's dead."

As the two stand in the weed-choked yard, sickly emaciated cats and kittens wander about, mewling. Many of them have crusty, infected eyes. Some wheeze audibly, further prompting Janice to persevere, "Seriously, I'm worried about their health."

"All my cats are fine. Go on now," Doris flares, "get out of here!" And she shoos Janice off her property.

"Why would anyone allow their animals to suffer," Janice muses. "Or why do they leave dead animals to rot in place? It bothered me that this behavior seemed just plain cruel. So when I took a psychiatrist out to evaluate, he determined that Doris suffers from a delusional disorder, and offered her medication, but she refused."

"Previously," Janice continues, "the SPCA warned Doris that her cats showed evidence of an upper respiratory illness that's highly contagious. When one feline gets it, it's easily spread throughout a neighborhood. Her neighbors, well aware of this, were frantic to stop its proliferation, but Doris still refused to cooperate."

In an attempt to avoid examining one's failure, the caretaker commonly refuses to accept reality. Possibly, Doris' inability to see the true condition of her cats stemmed from an unconscious attempt to avoid guilt. Should she recognize the unvarnished truth, she might experience extreme distress.

While tales of animal neglect confound and shock one and all, they're far too common. Animal control agencies cite the following hair-raising incidents: one woman crammed fifty dogs into a tiny, eight-by-ten-foot trailer; another fellow filled his home with dozens of sick and dying dogs, stacking their carcasses neatly in a closet; and in one case, an elderly woman died, leaving hundreds of cats to starve to death.

Exonerated murder suspect Edmund Burke, who had thirty live cats, kept the corpses of four dead ones in his refrigerator, explaining that he waited for the ground to thaw so he could bury them. In yet another Kafkaesque nightmare, more than 600 dogs and cats—believed to be an all-time record—were taken from a so-called animal rescue operation in Van Nuys, California; many were dead and others were so ill the authorities were forced to euthanize them.

Upon entry to the facility, animal cadavers were scattered about, other dead bodies were found beneath furniture, and the owner had even placed some in shopping bags. Officials described the conditions in this dwelling as unfit for animal or human.

Despite glaring evidence to the contrary, the owner of this non-profit insisted that the animals were healthy and well cared for, but *did* mention the inability to obtain a kennel permit due to zoning restrictions. Subsequent animal cruelty charges were filed and the proprietor was arrested.[5]

Euthanasia confronts animal hoarders with their worst nightmare: that someone has the right to take their beloved animals and put them to death is unfathomably galling. Yet, the individual in the aforementioned tale was unable to grasp that his neglect lay at the root of his animals' illness and suffering.

Animals are considered personal property, but ownership of a living creature should, at very least, be placed on par with that treasured *iPod*. This concept leads to the tale of the animal collector variously known as Vikki Rene Kittles, Susan Dietrich, Rene Depenbrock, and also as Lynn Zellan, who had a history of animal hoarding going back decades and her actions spanned multiple locales across the United States.

Ms. Kittles repeatedly evaded prosecution for animal cruelty by counter-suing veterinarians and the authorities, as well. This tactic flummoxed and frustrated many a community to the extent that each jurisdiction eagerly dismissed her case in exchange for her departure. One county even handed over gas money to ensure her speedy exit.

Upon landing in Oregon, Ms. Kittles refused to give her dogs heart worm medication and demanded that the veterinarian administer some sort of holistic treatment as an alternative. As a result, a legal battle ensued that dragged on so long that each dog died a painful death.[6]

While it's one thing to hoard inanimate objects, another dimension altogether unfolds when hoarding encompasses living creatures. So, invariably, when the rights of animal owners bump up against incidents of animal cruelty, matters become highly charged.

Bed and breakfast owner Elizabeth Blodgett is infamous among California pet protection agencies. Unable to care for the hundreds of animals that she'd amassed and housed on several of her properties in San Benito, Santa Cruz, and Santa Clara Counties, she was repeatedly charged with animal cruelty.

Back in 1981, 200 diseased dogs were removed from her Mountain View, California residence. The following year, fifty starving cats and dogs were scooped up from her beach-side resort in Capitola, also in California. And in 1986, 200 more dogs were rescued from filthy, overcrowded kennels at her San Juan Bautista ranch.[7]

Animal hoarding is a relatively new area of study, so mental health clinicians must basically wing it when confronted with the phenomenon. Yet a couple of psychiatric models attempt to understand the problem. The *delusional model* posits that hoarders of animals firmly believe that they, as previously stated, provide outstanding care for their pets, despite all material evidence to the contrary. Many see themselves as possessing immense empathic prowess as well as special abilities to communicate with animals.

The *dementia model,* as opined by animal researcher, Gary Patronek, identifies animal hoarding as a warning sign of early-stage dementia. This model emerged as a result of observing demented individuals who collect large numbers of animals and who also lack insight regarding their inability to attend to them.

One veterinarian noted that when his client was young and healthy, she provided excellent care for her cats, but as she aged, she became overwhelmed and her capacity to manage them markedly declined.

Eighty-four-year-old Sarah, who habitually feeds the neighborhood cats, asserts that it's her responsibility to do so. On the face of it, this shouldn't pose a problem, but Sarah squanders so much money on cat food that she lacks the financial wherewithal to feed herself.

Increasingly confused and disorganized, barely able to take care of herself, let alone several dozen cats, she's managed to collect a vast swath of neighborhood strays. At odds with her son Robert, who repeatedly calls animal control to trap and remove dead and dying animals, mother and son are not exactly on the best of terms. Despite their squabbles, the ever-dutiful Robert checks on his mum daily, bringing food and ferrying her to appointments.

Akin to gambling and other forms of substance abuse, there's the *addiction model* of animal hoarding, which holds that animal collecting indicates a lack of impulse control. Given a trajectory similar to the addict, the animal hoarder cannot resist and simply has to have one more pet. With their sole preoccupation centered around amassing, these people neglect most other aspects of their life, deny that any problems exist, and claim to be persecuted.

Here again, as researcher Dr. Gary Patronek notes, "Psychological trauma seems to be cropping up, such as losing a loved one or a chaotic childhood."

Indeed, animal hoarding may also be explained by the *attachment model* which hearkens back to an impaired childhood development that renders the hoarder incapable of forming close human bonds. Like the average person who hoards junk, these people replace human connection with animal bonding.

Given that many hoarders endured neglectful and/or abusive parents, the mere sight of a needy animal sets off a plethora of attachment issues so powerfully compelling that it gives rise to the compulsive urge to acquire it. Once acquired, since the hoarder has no experience with nurturing or caretaking, the animal receives little proper care or attention.

Though few in number and horrid to imagine, the *zoophilia model* is a category of animal hoarder who uses animals for sexual gratification. Kenneth Pinyan, although not necessarily a hoarder of animals, managed to die an ignominious death from injuries received during anal sex with a stallion. Known as the "Enumclaw Horse Sex Case," video footage of Pinyan and the horse became popularized by the film, *Zoo*.

There's good news, however: Pinyan's death prompted Washington State to pass a bill prohibiting sex acts with animals and the videotaping of the same. Currently, Washington law deems bestiality a Class C felony, punishable by up to five years in prison.[8]

Last, but not least, is the *OCD model,* which we've previously touched upon. Evidencing behaviors consistent with OCD, animal hoarders feel overwhelmingly responsible to prevent animals from harm, be that harm real or imagined, which compels them to engage in unrealistic or unnecessary attempts to protect them. Animal hoarding diverges from OCD-related hoarding, however, as repetitive, compulsive behaviors common to OCD don't manifest in precisely the same way with animal hoarders.

While the precise cause of animal aggregation may not always be clear, animal researcher Gary Patronek admonishes, "Public health professionals should recognize that animal hoarding may be a sentinel for mental health problems or dementia, which merit serious assessment and prompt intervention."

According to Patronek's 1999 study, in 69% of cases, animal feces and urine were found to have accumulated in the homes, and even in the beds of his subjects. Living with so many animals running roughshod results in poor sanitary conditions that cause the environment to deteriorate; a matter that can ultimately render the place uninhabitable. These squalid homes end up beyond repair and must be bulldozed.

When animals are out of control, neighbors are often first to note the problem. However, these people may be reluctant to make a fuss for fear of retaliation. When they *do* muster up courage to give authorities a call, the frequent lack of supportive response can infuriate. Of note, though: until matters tip into the realm of an acute public health or a mental health crisis, most government agencies are unable to act, as laws strictly limit when they can intervene. Even then, clear evidence of danger to the hoarder or to others must exist, and that threat must be imminent. Moreover, each government agency has specific parameters circumscribing when and how they can perform their functions.

Knowing when to intervene is tricky at best; jump in too soon and the individual's rights are violated. Wait too long and the outcome may be catastrophic. One gent burned to death inside his home before agencies could compile the legal paperwork to act.

Forcing a hoarder to change, even when legal authority is obtained, can also be catastrophic. According to Joanne Ostrom, LCSW, who runs packrat support groups, 25% of hoarders die from stress after a court order is issued to intervene. Made aware of the plan to extract her from her home, one elderly woman died of a heart attack the night prior.

Returning to the matter of animal hoarding: when a grievous situation finally *does* come to a head, the issue may fall within multiple jurisdictions that include public health, child welfare, zoning and building safety, animal and vector control, sanitation, police and fire, APS, animal protection, mental health, along with the Public Guardian, and the county's legal counsel.

Concern with regard to the spread of contagion and other health hazards prompts some communities to automatically monitor residents who husband large numbers of animals. To that end, laws may limit the number of pets permitted per household. Animal breeders and multi-pet menageries balk at such restrictions, asserting that government should butt out of their personal business. That being said, private business becomes public when it threatens community health and safety.

The owning or housing of numerous pets doesn't necessarily indicate mental instability. Many who have charge of large numbers of animals *do* provide adequate care, and plenty of humane animal rescuers safely shelter numerous cats and dogs until a home is found for them.

When animal cruelty is suspected, however, the Society for Prevention of Cruelty to Animals (SPCA) or the Humane Society are the go-to agencies to rescue or to trap endangered animals. Some states invite any citizen who believes an animal is being harmed to spearhead an application for a search warrant. Authorities then enter a dwelling to assess the situation, and at-risk animals are scooped up and taken into custody.

Animal cruelty is a crime, generally considered a misdemeanor punishable by fines. Counties force compliance by issuing citations and, if they exist, also cite building code and public health violations.

Shockingly, the first child abuse cases in this country were prosecuted under animal welfare statutes because no child protection laws existed at that time. Back then, raids to evaluate neglected animals shed light on situations involving deplorable child care, specifically incidents of abuse and neglect. Even nowadays, animal control officers may be the first to detect such incidents, for animal rights laws allow SPCA staff far greater latitude to enter a home without the owner's consent.

Finding a balance between compassion with regard to the animal hoarder's challenges and justice can be complicated, yet the priority for animal rescue staff is to save distressed animals. When initially arrived on the scene, the

SPCA seeks to elicit the hoarder's cooperation, urging the voluntarily reduction of the number of animals and improved quality of their care.

"Go slow to build rapport," advises Cynthia, a staffer at the Santa Cruz SPCA in California. "Rush things, and you blow it. When you take time to build rapport, the animal collector is able to hear your point of view and may find it tolerable to let their pets go."

Cynthia offers further pointers for those who work with animal hoarders. "By showing interest and conversing about their pets," she notes, "it's easier to gain trust and cooperation."

Acknowledging the collector's attempts to provide decent care, and noting the special bond they have with their critters can help break down barriers. Anticipate the hoarder's denial and don't argue about lapses in care or their insensitivity to the suffering of their pets. Also, don't badger them to change their behaviors. Arguing and trying to convince these people to see the error of their ways only serves to alienate. Most aren't deceitful or evil; they simply lack insight.

Cynthia further suggests that those who intervene ask practical questions, such as: *Can you afford pet food? Are you able you take the animals to the vet when needed? Do you have difficulty sleeping or eating due to the crowded conditions?* Innocuous probing invites the pet owner to divulge how they are coping, and to perhaps admit that they're overwhelmed.

Helping animal collectors problem-solve regarding their capacity to care for their pets also models positive behaviors. Often, the animal hoarder is happy to discuss non-threatening matters and may open up as a result. During these conversations, animal care staff can perform a rudimentary assessment, evaluating the hoarder's welfare and competence in order to make further referrals to other agencies.

"Build a safety net beneath the hoarder," Cynthia advises, "by getting their permission to enlist support of a friend or neighbor on their behalf. You might then ask that support person to keep an eye out and inform Adult Protective Services in the event that matters deteriorate or if a crisis arises."

"When I see appalling living conditions," Cynthia concludes, "it's easy to judge the owner as callous and neglectful. But still, I try to find a way to understand."

In the event that the hoarder resists recommendations to improve life for their acutely endangered animals, the only recourse that seems to bear gravitas is to prosecute them. This move shifts the issue from a mental or a public health venue to the criminal justice system. In such an instant, the hoarder may be prohibited from owning animals for a specified interval. Additionally, community service, along with perpetrator education that emphasizes proper animal care and humane values, can be required. In extreme cases, a court-ordered psychiatric evaluation and psychiatric medication may be imposed.

In repeated situations of animal abuse and neglect, the hoarder may serve jail time. Ongoing court-ordered monitoring is another means of keeping animal collecting in check. Infrequently, the perpetrator is placed under guardianship, and possibly forced to move into supervised living such as a board and care or a group home.

While undergoing prosecution there are times when the hoarder moves out of the area, as previously noted with Kittles. When they relocate, they merely resume collecting animals over again. One such woman purchased a new home every few years after each animal-laden residence turned to shambles.

Back to Doris with the myriad number of cats: "Sadly," Janice recounts, "Doris had zero interest in cooperating with animal welfare. Suspiciously defiant toward everyone who dared express concern, she vehemently denied that her cats were ill. Despite allegedly valuing her cats, she risked her own well-being as well as theirs, and could care less that her negligence posed a likely death sentence to other felines in the neighborhood.

"Although Doris refused to allow me or anyone else to enter her house," Janice goes on to note, "given its external appearance—the broken windows and the sagging, leaky roof—conditions inside posed a no-brainer."

Over the years, Doris' neighbors, their yards steadily overrun with her sickly cats, searched for compassionate, creative ways to resolve their differences. Ultimately, in light of her resistance, they enlisted the SPCA to trap, neuter, and administer medical treatment to her ailing strays at their own expense. Also, they offered to clean up her yard, which she refused.

At one point, the fire department was called to extinguish a blaze started in her carport by a homeless person she'd invited to camp there, and during that incident they managed to gain access inside. Later, they described the debris-filled scene.

Aside from cats urinating and defecating on everything, Doris' flea and cockroach infested home had no electricity, no refrigeration, nor working plumbing, and no trash collection. The roof leaked and sagged badly, and the chimney was cracked and leaning. Quite literally, the house appeared to be falling down around her.

"When we approached Doris' daughter, asking her to help," notes Janice, "she accused the County of stirring up trouble and of trying to take her inheritance."

At odds with public officials, the daughter rigorously blocked the County's efforts to intervene, even their attempts to make her mom's living situation tolerable. "My Mom isn't the problem, you are! All you [public officials] want is to foreclose on her property," she hollered when reached by phone, and then proceeded to rationalize her mother's behaviors as *uniquely creative*.

Matters came to a head the day Doris threatened to harm a neighbor. When police arrived, she came at the officer, flailing a pair of garden shears. In short order, she was hospitalized, placed under court-ordered guardianship, then sent to a care facility. The SPCA was then able to trap many of the cats, and the County red-tagged, and ultimately bulldozed her home.

A year later, still in a nursing home, when asked how she felt about her current living situation, Doris retorted, "I'm happy here and never want to leave!"

She then shot a sly grin. "What would *really* make me happy, though, would be to have me some more cats….Just a few of them."

CHAPTER 7

Evolution Gone Gonzo—Contributing Factors and Hoarding Research

---

"Between stimulus and response there is space. In that space is the power to choose our response. In our response lies our growth and freedom."

—Viktor Frankl

WHILE IT'S EASY TO UNDERSTAND someone who adores a pride of cats, it's tough to grasp the enormity of the hoarder's passion for junk mail or their willingness to risk eviction thanks to mountains of empty, grease-laden food containers. Hoarders themselves are often mystified as to their own actions, yet deep, intense love for their trash compels them to carry on.

On the other hand, the average collector is happily and healthily obsessed with their collection—be it Aboriginal art, or the aggregation of precious saintly relics—and generally, there's a sensible order to the process. Whether one collects porcelain dolls or postage stamps, as opposed to military ribbons, baseball cards, Steiff teddy bears or ugly beer mugs—there's an amazing variety of objects that can engage and fascinate.

So why do we collect?

Werner Muensterberger's book *Collecting: an Unruly Passion* uses the author's psychoanalytic mindset to examine the human, never-ending longing for yet another collectible. In the process, he concludes that collecting, as a need-driven compensatory behavior, gives rise to a sense of omnipotence.[1]

Likely, psychiatrist Erich Fromm would identify our propensity to collect, as well as to hoard, as one of the four basic ways in which humans adjust, albeit sometimes unproductively, to life. And Sigmund Freud actually *did* posit that collectors as well as hoarders, exhibit "anal" type characteristics.

Suspicious and reserved by nature, the anal personality, or the anal-retentive, tends to be excessively orderly, a behavior that Freud attributes to a fixation with regard to the rigors and conflicts that arise during toilet-training. While hoarders *do* fixate on collecting, Freud's notion falls away as it becomes clear that the meticulously neat anal-retentive in no way resembles the hoarder's sloppily, haphazard lifestyle.

Still, Freud's well known assertion that compulsions caused by deep-rooted emotional conflict are performed as defenses against unconscious, hostile, or sexual impulses that derive from the pre-oedipal, anal, and sadistic stages of psycho-sexual development bears merit with regard to the hoarder. Translated for our purposes: compulsive behaviors preoccupy the hoarder's attention to such an extent that their activities help to distract from disturbing memories or upsetting thoughts.

While a strict upbringing, an unresolved oedipal complex, or rigorously hygienic demands instilled during childhood cannot be deemed the sole underpinnings of the hoarder's activities, my client, Mark, a thirty-four-year-old, single dad caused me to wonder. Mark's station wagon is crammed to the gills with tools, clothes, garbage, along with hundreds of tree sticks and branches that he compulsively collects. As a result, there's barely room at the driver's seat, let alone enough space alongside for his young son. With his home also in chaos, fretting about the impact of his lifestyle on his child, he sought my help to clean up his act.

As we work that first day, Mark grows agitated and repeatedly insists on taking breaks. "My father," he explains, "ever-conscious as to what the neighbors thought, constantly preached the importance of cleanliness and of keeping organized. As a result, our lives were spic-and-span tidy, alright!

"That said, I'm pretty sure nobody suspected what went on behind closed doors. Calling us hideous names, he beat us senseless. So now," Mark quakes with fury as he continues, "if I keep everything organized, it's like I'm giving in to that bastard, and to society's false values."

Job finished, house and car now immaculate, Mark is of two minds: in part, he's pleased that he and his son can enjoy such tidy, comfy spaces, but he's also chagrined that he's given in to the expectations of his monster of a parent.

So it's no surprise that six months later Mark's car and home regress.

Applying Janice's term, Mark's actions and life experiences suggest another worthy case of "revenge clutter."

Yet the converse is may also arise. Adverse childhood circumstances can create a powerful drive for positive achievements and outcomes. At life's onset, with few-to-no advantages, Presidents Bill Clinton and Barack Obama elevated themselves by will, smarts, and luck. Likely, the reader knows others who've come from difficult or poor origins, yet managed to achieve well above and beyond the ordinary.

At first blush, I assumed that hoarding was engendered by a mentality of scarcity that became anchored in place by past trauma: be it the Holocaust, the Great

Depression of the 1930s, an atrocity or a genocide, or the enduring of abuse and neglect—events that might prompt the sufferer to stockpile...just in case.

Jodin, a resistance fighter during World War II, is a consummate saver of insignificant pieces of twine. Who knows why she has this particular focus; perhaps the possession of some nondescript piece of string once meant the difference between extinction and survival.

Turns out, my novice assessment of scarcity as a primary reason to hoard is debatable. Dr. Randy Frost, who explores this issue notes, "One of our first hypothesis when we began studying this problem was that it occurred in people who suffered from some form of material deprivation in childhood. In the first study we found no support for this hypothesis."[2]

In subsequent studies, he found a slight trend in that people with hoarding problems reported material deprivation, or endured traumatic events, or experienced childhood abuse—including forced sexual relations—but it was not enough of a clear trajectory to suggest that these experiences were causative.[3] Echoing Frost's comments, it bears note that younger generations who haven't endured significant lack tend to hoard as avidly as those forced to scrimp and to go without.

⌂⌂ ⌂

Which brings us to the next question: *Does the profile of a typical hoarder exist?*

As researchers, Dr. Frost and Dr. Gross report, hoarders are often unmarried, and if married, they're likely to divorce. I soon found that, although these folks hail from varied educational backgrounds, occupations, and socioeconomic status, hoarders tend to be older individuals with limited household incomes.

These folks span a broad spectrum of personality traits; many of them are miserly, stubborn, and obsessively controlling, while others are generous-hearted. Most *do* tend to be disorganized, exhibit self-neglectful behaviors, and live in squalor.[4]

While little is known about gender-specific differences between individuals who hoard, a study done in 2008 reports that, among female patients who attended an OCD clinic, those who hoarded had an earlier age of onset of OCD, as well as a greater severity of OCD symptoms. Many of women in the study were dual diagnosed with bipolar and panic disorders. Binge-eating, as well as alcohol and substance abuse impacted these participants, as well. Among men, a prevalence of social phobia was also noted.[5]

Diversity notwithstanding, while most hoarders tend to view their possessions as an extension of themselves, the basis for their attachment can vary. For some, their fixation stems from a *fear-based mentality;* their accumulations serve as symbols of safety. Without their stuff they feel exposed, anxious, and vulnerable. For others, the bond is *grief-based;* the thought of getting rid of anything, even a mere scrap of paper, prompts intense grief. *Guilt-based* hoarders worry in the extreme lest any item be wasted. *Sentiment-based* hoarders hang onto everything in hopes that their stuff will help them remember important events; possessions seen as are part of their history and therefore as an aspect of themselves. Discard anything and they feel diminished. A single hoarder can embody only one, several, or all of these attachment underpinnings.

Initially, mental health professionals simply thought that all obsessive-compulsive disorders were the result of bad parenting or were due to personality deficits. While the precise cause of OCD hoarding is still unclear, evidence certainly suggests that hoarding behaviors don't simply result from free will that's gone rogue.

"People with this [hoarding] problem tend to have a first-degree relative who also does," says Dr. Frost. "So it might be genetic, or it might be a modeling effect."[6]

Early hoarding studies indicate that hoarding runs in families; 50% to 80% of people who hoard have first-degree relatives who are considered to be hoarders. "In a more stringent test of the family connection," further notes Sanjay Saxena, Director of the University of California's Obsessive-Compulsive Disorders Program, "the Johns Hopkins OCD Family Study diagnosed hoarding among 12% of first-degree relatives of people who hoarded. Although this number is lower than the self-reported frequency found in other studies, it's significantly greater than that of relatives of people with ordinary OCD (3%). Other evidence indicates that hoarding is genetically influenced."[7]

While these data suggest a genetic link, Dr. Randy Frost adds comment, "On the other hand, modeling of parents' hoarding behavior may be a distinct possibility,"[8]—meaning, that hoarding behaviors may also be learned, and are not necessarily simply inherited.

Gene research *does* note that a marker on chromosome 14 is found in families who hoard. Sanjay Saxena, who has found that this genetic markers is specifically associated with compulsive hoarding, comments in an article in the *American Journal of Medicine*, "Other studies have confirmed that compulsive hoarding is strongly familial." This research "adds to mounting evidence indicating that compulsive hoarding is an etiologically discrete phenotype."[9]

Surgical introduction of lesions to a specific portion of the rat's brain causes them to cut down on the hoarding of food. Taking a leap: since food hoarding has a specific focal point in the animal's brain, the same just might be true for humans—that the genesis of human hoarding may derive from a distinct brain locale, as well.[10]

⌂⌂ ⌂

The proverb, "You can lead a horse to water…" got a substantial makeover when writer Dorothy Parker reworked it to read, "You can lead a horticulture, but you can't make her think." Repeatedly, this quandary is borne out while working with hoarders: While one can force the hoarder to tidy up, it's impossible to force them to stay clean.

In one fascinating pilot study, ten compulsive hoarders received a series of home visits to assess their living conditions, then they subsequently engaged in clutter removal practice sessions. After this training interval, participants reported a 15% reduction in clutter and a 50% reduction in their acquisitive activities. The study's intent was five-fold: to assist the hoarder to carve out an uncluttered area in the home; to increase appropriate use of that space; to improve decision-making skills involved in keeping their stuff organized; to refrain from further acquisition; and to discard or recycle unneeded items. According to participant self-report, all goals were successfully met.

From the outset, all these subjects expressed a keen desire to cooperate and to improve their circumstances. Despite alleging positive intentions, however, at study's end all participants continued to exhibit marked indecision to the extent that, rather than discard, they merely procrastinated. In terms of self-assessment, they also inflated their improvements. Actual outcomes based on objective measurement, as compared with clinical assessment of change, were poor.[11]

This resistance is borne out in another study where hoarders cooperated with great reluctance, for they sought help only at the insistence of their significant other. Their ensuing activities and perspectives tended to be egosyntonic, meaning their behaviors, values, and feelings closely matched their idealized self-image. Consequently, despite a stated desire for help, participants exhibited entrenched denial, rationalized their actions, passively resisted treatment, and procrastinated about fulfilling assignments that required them to alter their behaviors.

According to yet another 1990 study in which all participants were hoarders with OCD, every one of them lacked insight, weren't the slightest bit distressed by their behaviors. and made no attempts to refrain from collecting. They *did,* however, resist intervention and tried to keep their activities a secret. Unconcerned with regard to the unwieldy enormity of their collections, they tended to blame others for their hoarding-related problems.[12]

Then there's research published in the *Archives of General Psychiatry* by David Tolin of the Institute of Living in Hartford, Connecticut, which involved 107 participants. Recruited to receive brain scans using magnetic resonance imaging (MRI), 43 of the subjects were hoarders, 31 had other forms of OCD, and 33 others served as normal controls.

Assured that nothing would be thrown out against their wishes, subjects were asked to bring a bunch of their junk mail or newspapers to the lab. As the MRI was administered, participants were shown images of their own stuff or papers that weren't theirs, then asked if they wished to keep or shred these materials.

No surprise, the hoarders kept more of their own items than did those with OCD. As participants who hoarded contemplated tossing out or keeping each item, their brain responses differed from that of other participants. Excessive activation in the anterior cingulate cortex—a region of the brain involved with decision-making, particularly in situations that include conflicting information or uncertainty—was noted. This same region also impacts motivation, as well as the ability to focus attention and regulation of emotion. Brain activity was also noted to be heightened in the insula, a region that predominantly monitors one's emotional and physical states (it's also involved in disgust, shame, and other strong negative emotions). Together, these areas of the brain help humans to assign relative levels of importance or significance to objects.

Curiously, when the hoarders in the study made decisions about discarding junk mail that didn't belong to them, they again showed unusual activation of the anterior cingulate cortex and insula, but this activity was notably far lower than the norm for them. Furthermore, these subjects took a lot longer to decide whether to discard their possessions, and expressed feelings of sorrow and anxiety in the process.[13]

Michael Jenike, an OCD expert and professor of psychiatry at Harvard, who wasn't associated with the aforementioned research, offers comment: "This study is very interesting as it demonstrates that brain regions associated with monitoring for errors under conditions of uncertainty are activated when hoarding patients are deciding whether or not to throw out personal items." Translation: hoarders assign so much value to their possessions that it's difficult to impossible for them to get rid of their stuff.[14]

Similar abnormal brain activity is also seen in patients with autism. Often disengaged from others, the autistic individual, somewhat like the hoarder, rigidly adheres to routine and also demonstrates obsessive behaviors. This *brain lethargy* may help explain the lack of motivation and poor insight frequently noted in hoarders, which may further clarify why these individuals can live amidst overwhelming clutter and piles of junk, but fail to clear it out or are even bothered by it.

Meanwhile, hyperactivity noted in the hoarder's brain as they try to discard renders them so anxiously overwhelmed that they cannot act. If we take this detail at face value, hoarders aren't inherently slobs: they simply struggle, mightily, to make simple decisions about getting rid of their stuff, yet find themselves crippled with the inability to act.

"Many things are unique and distinct about hoarding," notes Dr. Eric Hollander of the autism and obsessive compulsive disorder program at New York's Albert Einstein School of Medicine, who also was not associated with this research. Hollander goes on to suggest that trans-cranial magnetic stimulation (TMS)—a therapy that uses non-invasive electrical stimulation of the brain to treat depression—may work for people who hoard.[15] TMS has few adverse side effects and has proven invaluable for those unable to tolerate SSRIs.

Interestingly, other neuroimaging studies also identify a particular area in the human brain as impacting OCD. Positron Emission Tomography (PET) scans are used to visualize chemical reactions within the brain and, depending upon the activity performed, certain centers illuminate. So when OCD sufferers engage in their rituals, certain brain centers—specifically the basal ganglia and the fronto-orbital region, situated behind the forehead—show abnormal activity. Subsequent to ingestion of appropriate medications or following an interval of behavioral therapy, those same brains are reviewed by PET scan, and activity appears more normal.[16]

In support of the premise that a precise locale in the brain impacts hoarding, Judith Rapoport, author of the book *The Boy Who Couldn't Stop Washing*, tells the following tale: Out of the blue, Sal, a hard-working, happily married family man developed a compulsion to pick up trash and save it. So zealous was he, that his collecting consumed so much of his time, he could not hold down a job, and he soon filled his home with junk. Despite his wife's protestations, including threats to leave him, Sal couldn't contain himself.

Ultimately, after undergoing psycho-surgery involving the severing of connections between the frontal lobes and deeper portions of his brain, Sal lost interest in collecting. Although his lobotomy effectively removed his compulsions, unfortunate personality changes replaced them, including a propensity to pinch women when out and about and prompted him to urinate in public places.[17]

As neurologist Oliver Sacks points out, a viral attack can have an adverse impact upon varied portions of the brain.[18] Which begs the question: *Did a virus, or a tumor, or some sort of biochemical change suddenly turn Sal into a hoarder?*

Related to this, Rapoport also mentions a 22-year-old man driven to suicide by his incessant compulsion to wash. This miserable fellow put a gun in his mouth, pulled the trigger, but miraculously survived. Not only did he survive, but his urge to wash abruptly departed.

The bullet, it seems, lodged in the left frontal lobe of his brain, effectively lobotomized him. By accident he managed to perform the same operation that cured Sal. Yet his tale has a happier outcome; this young man went on to attend college and led a normal life.[18]

Other individuals have been known to to incur a brain injury, be it head trauma or a cerebrovascular accident, and then engage in OCD hoarding. Such behaviors that emerge subsequent to incurring traumatic injury or a lesion to the brain suggest that there's a biological basis for hoarding,[19] and the aforementioned imaging studies help document the activation of specific brain regions in those with OCD hoarding.[20]

⌂⌂ ⌂

The idea that a genetic etiology for hoarding exists is also supported by evidence of hoarding behaviors seen in genetically-based disorders such as Prader-Willi Syndrome (PWS) and Velocardiofacial syndromes.[21,22] The hallmarks of Prader-Willi Syndrome include excessive food consumption, as well as poor muscle tone, and also include OCD behaviors such as hoarding, arranging, and ordering of objects. Velocardiofacial syndrome is a genetic condition that's often hereditary, which is characterized by a combination of medical problems that can include: cleft palate, or an opening in the roof of the mouth; malformed and/or poorly functioning kidneys; a characteristic facial appearance; learning problems; speech and eating problems; and heart defects. Compulsive behaviors, including hoarding are common among these individuals. Additionally, there's genetic link to specific chromosomal regions seen in families with OCD.[23] However, definitive understanding as to why hoarding occurs in these syndromes have yet to fully come to focus.

Neurological disorders, including epilepsy and chorea—which involves jerky, involuntary movements—impact certain portions of the brain and may also result in obsessive-compulsive behaviors, including hoarding.[24]

Aside from showing up as an OCD behavior, hoarding may also exist as a symptom of bipolar illness. Bipolar, also known as manic-depression, may include making manic, compulsive purchases, in tandem with difficulty controlling urges that cause one to collect and keep rubbish.

A small percent of schizophrenics also hoard; yet typically, their focus revolves around fixed beliefs or delusions. Driven by bizarre thoughts, including hallucinations and magical thinking, Mario, a man with schizophrenia, exhibits extreme emotional reactions—including intense sorrow, anxiety, fear, and panic, along with the occasional violent outburst—that focus on the need to protect his hoard.

One sibling duo crammed their home with newspapers and trash to protect from harmful, gender-changing radiation. That they shared the same delusion is unusual in and of itself, yet despite their shared lifelong mindset, they both welcomed life-changing help.

Marcie, too, fears she'll be harmed by radiation, so she gathers up garbage, filling her home to insulate. Her windows are tacked, inches deep, with sheets of newsprint, which she claims helps to protect from harmful emanations. Rain or shine, she also never ventures out without donning hat, galoshes and London Fog raincoat. For added protection, she sleeps amidst balled-up newspapers that fill her home, floor to ceiling. For heat, she keeps the kitchen burner continually lit, which is a dangerous combination. When wafting papers ignited, she nearly burnt to death as she slept.

Alcoholics and, to a lesser extent, drug abusers, may hoard. In both cases, clutter accumulates secondary to inertia caused by the haze of drink or the anhedonia of depression. Empty bottles strewn about comprise the bulk of this group's stash.

Stanley, an alcoholic, lived alone, surrounded by dozens of cats. When he drank himself to death, his family shoveled out piles of unprocessed mail, along with whiskey bottles and beer cans by the thousands. Additionally, Stanley managed to aggregate several hundred Hawaiian shirts and had a humongous collection of old, rare comic books, probably worth thousands.

According to relatives, Stan was hard to like and difficult to know. "As we cleared his home," notes his sister-in-law, "I realized, although Stan didn't exhibit typical compulsive behaviors, he fought depression all his life, and used his stuff to insulate from pain. Likely, his drinking and collecting helped keep his suffering in abeyance."

△△ △

We all have a favorite Auntie who once kept her home in pristine order, but the place has succumbed to filth and trash. Of previous note, such decline may signal early-stage dementia. Dementia may also occur as result of several diseases, including Alzheimer's, vascular dementia, dementia with Lewy-Bodies, Parkinson's, fronto-temporal, and mixed dementia, which is a combination of one or more of the aforementioned. Dementia resulting from physical brain changes causes loss of memory and deterioration of other mental functions and is progressive; meaning, it worsens over time.

While people experience the stages of dementia differently, most share a similar constellation of symptoms. Mental and physical deterioration largely depends upon the underlying cause. For some, dementia progresses rapidly. For others, it may take years to reach an advanced stage. When cognitive capacity is diminished, the demented hoarder has trouble performing sequential tasks, which in turn impairs their ability to decide what to discard, or how to sort, clean, or organize.

According to a study of 133 dementia patients, 22.6% exhibited hoarding behaviors.[25] Put another way, hoarding among those with dementia is common; an estimated one in four, and in some studies, one in five demented persons accumulate and keep paraphernalia. Unlike the average hoarder, though, those with dementia exhibit little to no distress when their possessions are discarded.

Should the demented hoarder also happen to be paranoid or delusional, they may be given to confabulation, which means they fill in memory gaps with confused and confusing explanations. To complicate already complex matters, whether caused by vulnerability or by innate paranoia, often the demented hoarder believes that others steal from them.

George, a schizophrenic hoarder with dementia, steadfastly insisted that two men showed up every Friday, demanding that he pay them $200 in cash. Always, he described the duo as garbed in red Pendleton shirts, and mentioned their diminutive stature.

To accommodate their demand, George went to the bank weekly to extract the money they demanded; a routine that spanned well over ten years. While most chalked George's story up to hallucinatory delusions, an acquaintance happened to stop by his house one day and interrupted two short-statured men, garbed in screaming-red Pendletons.

"After that," Janice notes, "every client tale—be it far-fetched or credible—I automatically accept as fact until evidence suggests otherwise."

Dysthymia, a term applied to those with low-grade, chronic sadness, is commonly noted in those who hoard. Living in a heavily cluttered environment, coupled with a dearth of coping skills, add a dollop of low motivation, and the inability to focus, and how can the hoarder possibly get organized?

Significantly, findings from a study using an undergraduate sample suggest that indecisiveness may be a major underlying feature of hoarding. These results further suggest that hoarding is not just confined to the OCD spectrum.[26]

What to save and how to organize is beyond the pale for most hoarders. These folks fret that an item won't be available at some later date, so they insist that they need to hold onto it—*it* being something incredibly obscure or redundant—no matter how remote the possibility of its future use. Rather than mistakenly jettison something, these people avoid distress by hanging onto everything.

With the tendency to see her possessions as an extension of self, Maxine gets agitated and yells at her house cleaner for merely dusting stuff off. Much like a child engaged in magical thinking, as previously remarked, she lives in fear that something terrible will happen if she even stirs up her posessions. Furthermore, should she cease to collect, she believes the outcome would be catastrophic. Although she acknowledges that her collecting causes major life dysfunction and is a source of shame, she reports seismic levels of anxiety at the mere thought of discarding.

Its heartening to note that hoarding research is ongoing. Recently, a call for subjects went out from researchers at the University of California at San Francisco who've teamed up with the Mental Health Association of San Francisco as they seek to learn more about the relative efficacy of different forms of treatment. Specifically, some participants will engage in peer-facilitated support groups, while others will receive cognitive behavioral therapy.[27]

Since it's now known that hoarding originates from abnormal brain function, not from laziness, its identification as a bonafide illness—rather than a matter of personal choice—allows a modicum of consolation for sufferers and can help engender the compassion of family and friends.

CHAPTER 8

Look, Ma, No More Stuff!—Therapeutic Treatments for Hoarders

Disposophobia: *The scientific term used in the DSM-V to describe hoarding, specifically the excessive fear of discarding one's possessions.*

—the Diagnostic and Statistical Manual of Mental Disorders

Historically, the antidote for compulsive-disorders—once thought to be the result of possession by evil spirits—was an old-fashioned exorcism. The Greeks, followed by other civilizations, also enjoyed treating their obsessive-compulsives with strong cathartics. Although rarely employed these days, the cingulotomy—a surgical procedure that involves incising tiny lesions between the frontal lobe and deep cortical structures of the brain—can interrupt those annoyingly hyperactive circuits. A little snip here, an itsy snip there, and voila...no more Bloomingdale's sales!

Should friends and family want to help the hoarder organize, a massive spring cleaning cannot resolve the problem. While the knee-jerk reaction of fed-up family members, as well as that of friends and neighbors, is to rent a dumpster and toss out the mess, true resolution is far more complex.

Removing stuff without the hoarder's consent may resolve the problem in the short term, but aside from helping to sharpen resistance, it does nothing to alter their ongoing behaviors. See, it's critical for hoarders to truly opt for recovery—meaning, they must actively invest in ceasing to collect—and further, they need to be willing to learn discernment.

To take over robs them on all fronts and is a sure-fire way to frustrate all parties involved. Moreover, chucking stuff out risks alienating them. So it's best to remove a hoarder's possessions without their consent only when the situation is dire.

△△ △

Based on anecdotal evidence as well as clinical studies, as already known, obsessive-compulsive hoarders respond poorly to medication and to treatment. "Whereas most people with OCD are aware that their behavior is out of control, OCD hoarders usually lack insight or don't think that it's that unusual," notes Dr. Saxena, director of UCSD, OCD Clinic. "Inevitably, it's family members or friends who bring them in for therapy, and they're unusually difficult to treat."[1]

Dr. Gillette, psychiatrist for Santa Cruz County in California, echoes Dr. Saxena's sentiments. "Commonly, a hoarder comes up with all kinds of reasons why they cannot part with an object. 'I'm saving this box for my grandchildren,' or 'I love literature and will someday read that book,' or 'Even though this food is outdated, it's still edible, so I'll hold onto it.' Superficially, some of these explanations make sense, but the hoarder finds any excuse to save everything."

Trying to reason is a waste of breath. All logic mustered can't induce a hoarder to stop, and it's counterproductive to argue or to shame the hoarder into changing. To threaten or insist that that they transform their lifestyle merely increases secrecy. Besides, when pushed too hard, the hoarder cuts off contact and isolates.

How, then, does a hoarder get help?

There are two main types of treatment for hoarding, specialized cognitive-behavioral therapy (CBT) and medication. We'll discuss both these topics shortly. As we know, however, without coercion of some kind, be it from loved ones or threat of eviction, clutter reduction rarely happens on a voluntary basis. Should the hoarder actually agree to clean up, it's critical that they recieve ongoing support to maintain a clutter-free environment.

If the individual actually gets down to discarding, family and friends may hope for an immediate change, but change cannot be forced. For a long-lasting shift to occur, the hoarder must learn how to make decisions about their possessions at a pace they can tolerate, and should they enlist help, it's critical to respect their wishes.

There's good news; treatments specifically aimed at hoarding now meet with far greater success than they did a few years ago. For the intervention espoused by Dr. Randy Frost and his colleagues to stick, a three-pronged approach seems best. Ingestion of an anti-anxiety medication, in partnership with undertaking CBT, while learning practical organizational skills effectively covers the bases.

CBT enables one to uncover and examine unhealthy beliefs and activities, and then replace them with healthier, more constructive behaviors and beliefs. According to Gail Steketee, however, the CBT therapist must first help the client recognize that a problem actually exists.

To that end, subjects in one study involving packrats and chronic savers complained of great difficulty locating possessions, and acknowledged shame and family conflict due to their activities. With most lamenting the inability to invite guests into their homes, these eighteen participants divulged that their previous efforts to cease to collect on their own had failed and were actually eager to receive help.

At study's outset, each participant underwent a baseline brain scan, Next, they engaged in CBT with an emphasis on *exposure* and *flooding* practices. *Exposing* themselves to the feared object, while in a secure, controlled environment, made it easier for them to grapple with, and to manage their anxiety. *Flooding* then required prolonged exposure to whatever agent or circumstance happened to trigger their compulsions, be it the sight of a yard sale or a dumpster.

Deliberately igniting their obsessions, while simultaneously stopping themselves from performing the attendant compulsions, the subjects then inserted wholesome, enjoyable behaviors in their stead. Some suggested enjoyable behaviors included the refocusing of attention onto a hobby or participating in a physical endeavor. Meditation offers another way to self-soothe, and volunteering or executing a kindly act are other examples.

The upshot: twelve of the study's eighteen participants experienced dramatic, long-lasting reduction of symptoms. On follow up, positron emission tomography (PET) demonstrated notable changes in brain chemistry for all participants. Researcher Jeffrey Schwartz and his UCLA colleagues further noted: the more impressive the behavioral changes, the greater the PET scan shift.[2]

These people weren't cured; they still faced ongoing struggles to maintain their gains. Yet this exciting study points out the persuasive power of thought and its impact on behavior—that deliberately directed thinking *can* and *does* alter brain function.[3]

It bears note that insight alone was insufficient to evoke change, but action involving the substitution of an alternative behavior, while refraining from performing the compulsive act, *did* cause transformation. Translation: hoarders can directly influence their behaviors by interrupting the urge to collect, which in turn eventually weakens the compulsion over time, thereby solidifying the circuitry of resistance.

Should the hoarder move from resistance to actually seek help, and before treatment can begin, a physician or psychiatrist must perform an intake assessment to establish a precise clinical diagnosis. To that end, a complete psychiatric history, along with a physical examination will help determine the possible presence of medical underpinnings. During this intake phase several co-existing diagnoses may be unearthed.

When several diagnoses exist, treatment is more complex. If the hoarder is schizophrenic, for example, their behaviors may become more refractory to treatment when an anti-psychotic medication is taken. Frustratingly, however, it's tough to talk someone who is paranoid, and may think the therapist is out to harm them, into taking medications.

Evidence of dementia and instances of low intellect can initially be ascertained through simple mental status testing and by evaluating client behavior. Further diagnoses are then confirmed through blood work and in-depth neurological evaluation.

Additional issues may complicate determination of a correct diagnosis. Such issues include alcoholism, the presence of a panic disorder or depression, the existence of autism, or Tourette's, as well as other OCD symptoms, and may also include OCD Spectrum Disorders. Eating disorders such as anorexia nervosa, as well as schizophrenia, or bipolar illness may also be part of the mix.

⌂⌂ ⌂

Selective serotonin re-uptake inhibitors (SSRI), a class of medications often used to treat OCD and OCD hoarding, impacts the hoarder's low levels of serotonin.[4] By blocking the reabsorption or reuptake of serotonin, more of it is made available to then fuel healthier brain function.

Serotonin is one of the chemical messengers (neurotransmitters) that carry signals between brain cells, and is responsible for balancing and maintaining mood. Low levels of serotonin lead to depression and engender a lack of impulse control, as well as difficulties with limit-setting, which can lead to destructive, compulsive behaviors.

The presence of greater amounts of serotonin in the brain helps ease depression, which in turn reduces symptoms of OCD. Another way to put it, serotonin acts as the *brakes of the brain*, lending support so that those afflicted can say "no" to collecting. Prozac (fluoxetine), Paxil (paroxetine), Zoloft (sertraline), Celexa (citalopram), and Luvox (fluvoxamine maleate) are commonly prescribed SSRIs.

While initial studies failed to find SSRI's effective in treating hoarders, Dr. Sanjay Saxena's work contradicts this. In research that included 32 compulsive hoarders who ingested the SSRI Paxil for 80 days, participants demonstrated "significant improvement" when subsequently tested for depression and anxiety.[5]

It can be tricky to find the proper dose of medication to achieve relief. If there's no improvement after taking a medication at the highest dose for at least twelve weeks, the physician may want to add a second medication or switch to another one. Examples of additional medications that can be of benefit include Risperdal (risperidone), Zyprexa (olanzapine), Seroquel (quetiapine), Haldol (haloperidol), and Abilify (aripiprazole). These antipsychotic drugs are typically used to treat schizophrenia, bipolar-mania, or autism.

Stepping further outside the SSRI box, the psychotropic Anafranil (clomipramine hydrochloride), which is structurally similar to a class of medications known as tricyclic antidepressants (TCAs), may be used to treat some OCD hoarders. Another classification that includes Effexor (venlafaxine) are the selective serotonin and norepinephrine reuptake inhibitors (SSNRIs) that also provide relief for some.

Should those medications fail to do the trick, other options exist. Monoamine oxidase inhibitors (MAOIs) are used to treat depression and panic. When ingesting MAOI's, one must refrain from eating foods that contain tyramine, a compound that naturally occurs in fermented comestibles such as cheese, beer and sour cream, as it can induce dangerously high blood pressure.

For those with a coexisting diagnosis of bipolar illness, taking Lithium (Eskalith and Lithobid), for example, also impacts serotonin levels. Several anti-anxiety medications such as Valium (diazepam), Klonopin (clonazepam), Ativan (lorazepam), and Xanax (alprazolam) may make it easier for the hoarder to part with their possessions. When taken long term, however, this class of medication, known as benzodiazepines, can cause abuse and addiction.

Drugs don't offer an instant fix and may initially be off-putting, as they may increase the very symptoms the sufferer wishes to avoid. SSRIs have side effects, including anxiety and the jitters, that can be similar to panic. Some medications also cause bowel upset, insomnia, tremors, and the sweats, and also knock out one's libido. The good news: usually the nasty side effects subside over time, but if not, the physician can change to a medication with a different side-effect profile.

When Marvin takes his medication Zoloft, he's less depressed and anxious, which then enables him to redirect his obsessive thoughts. This medication also improves his problem-solving skills, thereby heightening his ability to make decisions. Additionally, it gives him a modicum of self-control, which then helps to squelch his urge to collect. As a result, his wife Ingrid heaves a sigh of relief.

"Although I no longer collect, I don't much care for the medication's side-effects," he groans. "I sleep a lot and have turned into quite the fatty. Go without, though, and my missus says she'll leave me."

Another glitch; these medications may require four to six weeks to kick in. For reasons unknown, folks beset with OCD tend to take longer to experience improvement. Is is frequently seen that OCD patients also require a higher dose of SSRI medication to achieve the relief that tends to occur gradually over months.

Over time, I've come across a few self-help hints that serve as adjuncts to treatment. A daily session, sitting in front of full spectrum lighting can increase serotonin levels. Making dietary changes, including the ingestion of the amino acid tryptophan, helps supply the brain with proper fuel to create serotonin.

And the lowly potato contains insulin-producing carbohydrates which help transport tryptophan across the blood brain barrier.[6] Furthermore, inositol, a natural sugar, has proven to increase serotonin in several studies.[7]

Each brain is unique, so determining which medication is most effective may be a matter of trial and error. If one form of medication doesn't work, perhaps another will. Surprisingly, if a family member who hoards finds success taking a particular pill, there's no guarantee that it will be effective for another relative.

As mentioned, yet again, hoarders don't respond as well as other OCD sufferers do to medication or to behavioral therapy. "It tells us this may be a unique neurological subtype," explains Dr. Saxena, who headed a three-year study at UCLA to determine if obsessive-compulsive hoarders possess unique brain abnormalities. In this study, tomography scans—three-dimensional images of the internal structure of hoarder's brains—noted metabolic irregularities in participants' frontal cortices.

Dr. Saxena further comments, "Because these patients don't respond in the same manner to medicine, there's a likelihood that they may have different brain patterns than other OCDs, which will enable us direct our research into other drugs."[8]

For the most part, despite their lack of efficacy with regard to hoarding, medications remain the primary treatment for an OCD hoarder. Anti-anxiety medications help soothe, making it easier for the individual to discard their stuff. And all medications, when used in conjunction with therapy, serve as a bridge to ease the way for more deep-seated, long-lasting behavioral changes.

⌂⌂ ⌂

Ken Kesey's wild and crazy character, Randle Patrick McMurphy, the hero of *One Flew Over the Cuckoo's Nest*, fakes insanity to avoid doing time in prison. As an alternative sentence McMurphy lands in a mental hospital where a power struggle with the tyrannical Nurse Ratched ensues. As a result, McMurphy's brain is rearranged through a series of electroshock therapy treatments (ECT).

Lest one recoil in horror, despite ECT's controversial historical reputation, when employed for the severely depressed, who haven't achieved relief from other forms of treatment, it can be life-saving. Nowadays, the far more humane procedure involves painless application of electrical impulses to the temples. Although memory loss may occur, it's generally restored over time.

When all other efforts to improve her depression failed, Kitty Dukakis, wife of one time Presidential hopeful, Michael Dukakis, gave ECT a try. After her first treatment, she wrote, "I felt alive." Sixteen years later, with her brain still rebooted to positive effect, she continues to receive maintenance treatments about every two months.[9]

There is also brain surgery known as the cingulotomy. The cingulum, which acts as the conduit for communication of the limbic system, is responsible for long-term memory, along with the regulation of emotion and our sense of smell. Furthermore, it's where the ability to correct mistakes resides, and it's also the loci for the appraisal of pain.

Despite that jest about the cingulotomy at chapter's onset, to undergo this treatment is no laughing matter. Introduced in the 1940s, Russians used the bilateral cingulotomy to treat addiction and, albeit rarely, chronic pain. This procedure, eventually replacing the psycho-surgery known as a lobotomy, involves severing fibers of the cingulum bundle, and is used to treat severe, intractable depression, as well as extreme forms of OCD.

Lobotomies—frequently and zealously over-performed in the 1950s—resulted in tragic personality changes. Thankfully, these days the more judiciously applied procedure uses computer-aided technology to sever tiny nerve fibers with such precision that no personality alterations need occur.

△△ △

In addition to medications, behavioral therapies are know to successfully produce brain changes that specifically impact activity in the fronto-orbital region. Harvard psychiatrist Steve Hyman further notes that these therapeutic counseling sessions help amplify serotonin levels.[10]

Since research involving OCD hoarders reveals a biochemical imbalance, it's suggested that the brain is stuck in the "on" position ad nauseum. Ingesting certain medications while engaged in cognitive behavioral therapy

(CBT) helps soothe the over-stimulated brain by decreasing its hyperactive circuitry, thereby helping the hoarder to get unstuck.

What's more, brain imaging reveals that hoarders, as compared with non-hoarders, have slower glucose metabolism in their brains' cingulate gyrus and occipital cortices. These individuals show abnormally low baseline activity of the cingulate gyrus while at rest, and increased activation of that area and surrounding cortical regions while performing symptom-provoking tasks has also been noted. The posterior cortex, which is adjacent, regulates one's ability to choose between multiple conflicting options and controls spatial orientation, as well as episodic memory.

This finding has major ramifications, suggesting that compulsive hoarding, along with the hoarder's poor response to standard OCD treatment, may be caused by diminished and abnormal function of these areas. Saxena concludes,"Compulsive hoarding syndrome appears to be a discrete entity, with a characteristic profile of core symptoms that are not strongly correlated with other OCD symptoms, but show distinct susceptibility genes, as well as unique neurobiological abnormalities that differ from those in non-hoarding OCD."[11]

Further research at the UCLA Medical Center examined subjects before and after they engaged in CBT. At study's onset, when obsessive thoughts took an upswing, a flurry of activity in the orbital-cortex was seen. After an interval of therapy, participants showed demonstrably reduced activity in the aforementioned brain region, along with a concomitant reduction in OCD symptoms.[12] This result is far-reaching insofar as it suggests that OCD brain patterns *can* be altered with psycho-therapeutic treatment.

△△ △

So what, exactly, does cognitive-behavior therapy consist of?

"To properly address the cognitive distortions associated with hoarding, it is essential to first define the emotions involved in the patient's attachment to possessions," notes Dr. Steketee.[13] To that end, it's believed that hoarding stems from several areas of emotional difficulty.

First off, as we know, hoarders have *trouble processing information,* and second, it's hard for them to make sensible *decisions as to how to organize* their stuff. With problem-solving capability as an enormous obstacle, the hoarder then avoids making decisions about everything.

Where should I put this new dish towel, and do I really need thirty of them? Pose head-scratchers for hoarders.

Further confounded by what's known as *under-inclusion,* packrats categorize their possessions so narrowly that objects can't be lumped together, and each item is believed to be irreplaceably unique. Should the individual try to sort or organize, they become so confounded they simply drop stuff in a heap.

Indeed, decision-making is an immense challenge for Norman, as he believes discarding is wasteful, even if he knows the object's intrinsic value is nil. According to his mindset, each empty McDonald's burger box is unique and holds great importance. As a result, he emphatically insists that it's a mistake to discard a single one of them, for he just might need it later. This means his living space is trash-filled, thereby rendering it uninhabitable.

Mere contemplation as to whether to discard induces white-knuckled panic, so he avoids discarding to avert regrettable mistakes. Incapable of divesting his possessions, despite risk of eviction, he keeps right on collecting, thereby creating stress-filled misery for himself.

As a third area of difficulty, hoarders are excessively emotionally *attached to their stuff*—this includes stinky, moldy trash that few others find endearing. While attachment to his photo-jammed scrapbook is understandable, Norman's excessive passion for those empty, food-encrusted boxes and the trash that he exhumes from the garbage defies logic.

In the short run, while collecting helps avert momentary distress, it ultimately causes him far bigger problems. When he's inevitably evicted, Norman will have to part with these things anyway and will undergo tremendous grief at the loss.

The fourth area of difficulty, hoarders tend to suffer from poor recall and they *mistrust their ability to remember.* Norman, too, doesn't trust his memory, which explains the scraps of paper that bulge from all pockets and the pen snugged behind his ear. His unwillingness to part with the written word takes the form of aggregated newspapers and food wrappings, all which contribute to his repeated evictions.

Challenging himself to retain every last detail of any paper he examines—an impossible task—he saves everything, even though he'll never get back to them. Fretting further, insisting that they may be needed for tax purposes, Norman saves all receipts; never mind that he hasn't filed a return in ages. Junk mail is also kept; tossing it out might mean the loss of a bargain. "I'd rather be safe than sorry," is his constant refrain.

As previously mentioned, a physician of Janice's acquaintance cannot bear to part with her medical journals. "I never know," notes this woman whom many hold in high regard, "when the very report that I've tossed out might save a patient's life. Consequently, articles and journals fill my garage to the extent that I cannot pull my car in. When I *do* go in search of information, it's rare that I can actually find it.

"By saving everything, I maintain the illusion that every [medical] detail is at my fingertips. Knowing that every scrap of is out in my garage—be it useful or not—helps to ease my mind."

While she's highly functional in so many other aspects of her life, keeping these journals has an adverse impact on her family. "Since our garage is unusable," she reports, "my spouse urges me to rent storage space. Oh...and guess what," she adds with a sheepish grin, "I also hoard e-mails and refuse to discard them...even the spam."

Another area of difficulty for hoarders, Norman included, is that they entertain *erroneous beliefs* about their possessions. In such instances, common refrains include the following: *If I don't save this piece of string or this box, I won't have it when I really need it.* Or, *If I don't buy 100 cans of soup and stash them, I just might run out and starve.*

Sandra, too, feels responsible for what might happen should she dispose of her humongous record and book collections. And heaven forbid that she ask her able-bodied sons to help her get rid of them! "They have no respect for the time and effort it took to amass my books, so I don't allow my boys to touch them, and I certainly won't pass any of them on until they appreciate what I've done for their sakes." Notably, her sons, in their mid-fifties, haven't the slightest interest in her collections.

As a sixth area of challenge, hoarders firmly believe they *must be prepared for every contingency*. Each week, Jodin, a brilliant engineer and W.W. II Resistance survivor, purchases several hundred pounds of meat at the market, then heads home with it in the back of her pickup. No worries about schlepping it inside to find freezer space; it remains in the truck-bed where it thaws and drips to make an oozing stink, causing neighbors to complain about the smell.

Jodin doesn't give a hoot about the waste and claims it's her God-given right to do as she pleases. Stating that she merely wants to have the meat on hand, flies buzz about, and dogs, rats, raccoons, skunks—animals of all stripes—scamper up to enjoy the booty.

Since she's created a fetid, cringe-worthy health hazard, arguments ensue between Jodin and her neighbors. Nasty words are flung and threats are made, resulting in calls to County mental and public health services to resolve the problem. The first time Janice drives up to pay a visit, the wafting, putrid scent greets her as she pulls up.

Keeping the hoarder's particular difficulties in mind, we now jump back to the CBT model. This mode of treatment doesn't involve ignoring or resisting tormenting thoughts, for the more one resists, the more powerful such thoughts become. And CBT doesn't consist of traditional *Talk Therapy*; to yak about the minutiae of one's problems doesn't necessarily help the hoarder to change.

CBT involves facing one's fears and figuring out how to live with the ongoing pesky obsessions, while learning not to let them run one's life. Treatment means exposure to techniques aimed at changing the hoarder's relationship to their preoccupations and compulsions, and may also include meditation and relaxation practices.

In essence, this is how it works: Patty stares down the object of her anxiety—in this case books—then examines her compulsions, including the reasons she's driven to hoard. Loneliness, fear of going without, and the opportunity to refocus away from her poor self-image give her pretext to collect. She then refrains from acting out her ritualized behaviors, which in her case means not buying books, and to thereby exert control to redirect her thoughts and urges. While her compulsive urges may persist as she repeatedly faces her fears, it's hoped that her attendant anxiety will dwindle, till eventually—best case scenario—she gains the upper hand.

All is not necessarily smooth-sailing, however. In reality, many a hoarder becomes too uncomfortable with the process to endure the ensuing changes.

With Dr. Randy Frost to the rescue, he espouses *Exposure and Response Prevention Therapy* (ERP), which combines behavior modification practices with cognitive restructuring.[14] Cognitive restructuring involves identifying irrational or maladaptive thoughts, known as *cognitive distortions*. Examples of distortions may include engaging in all or nothing thinking, or magical thinking, or overgeneralizing, as well as magnification.

Once a foundation is firmly established in therapy, the client sets out to face real life anxiety-producing situations. For example, the hoarder might take a saunter past a thrift store or go by a dumpster, but refrains from entering the shop or from peeking into the trash bin. Deliberate and repeated exposure to these triggering environs and situations, while avoiding acting out the accompanying urges, helps one's anxiety to gradually dissipate, till it no longer holds power. Jeffrey Schwartz, who further espouses his *15 Minute Delay Rule* notes that as these steps are mastered, the client's need for medication is also diminished.[15]

As we know, hoarders are often too embarrassed or in such denial that they neglect to discuss their proclivities to collect in counseling. Likely, they will only admit to depression, and should the topic of hoarding crop up, they will minimize its magnitude.

With this tendency in mind, the therapist should regard the client's downplaying or denial with skepticism, and respectfully press to unearth undisclosed behaviors. Clarifying why the individual is seeking help, while assessing their level of insight, helps clarify whether the client welcomes change or not. Without a modicum of sincere investment, treatment is a waste of time.

Motivation for most seems to stem from looming negative consequences. Threat of divorce, estrangement from family, social isolation, health concerns, impending eviction, or other legal sanctions are the most common concerns that propel the hoarder into treatment.

To be of utmost service, the counselor must ascertain how out of control and how much damage the hoarding causes. As rapport is built, gentle probing can help unmask the true nature and extent of the problem. If an impasse is reached, asking the client for the lowdown as to a typical day's activities may tease out additional details.

When possible, making a home visit brings a world of clarity. At very least, access to photos, inside and outside the house, can convey a mouthful.

A reachable treatment goal—one that hoarders will most likely accept—is to help them establish a patch of uncluttered living space. Sadly, although many a client verbally agrees to this, they tend to bristle and balk when it comes down actual discarding. Here's where it's handy to remind them why they've sought help.

Emphasis on the organizing of possessions as a means of improving one's lifestyle, as opposed to dwelling on the discharge of junk, can improve receptivity. For example, with increase of appropriate living space as a modest goal—*appropriate* being the operative word—many a hoarder is eager to access their stove-top or to use their bathtub.

By working to clear a discrete area of the house so it can be used for its intended purpose, allows new behavior patterns to emerge. With focus on the end result as its own reward, hopefully, the hoarder will be motivated to maintain any areas they've de-cluttered.

Success doesn't necessarily mean excavating the entire home. Clearing one room or tidying one small corner is pretty darn good!

As part of the process, the therapist should assist the client to identify and list all troubling thoughts or behaviors on note cards, which they then rank from easiest to most difficult. Taking the least problematic, least scary behavior first, the hoarder will identify one specific, realistically attainable goal.

Since Norman is swimming in mail, he might set a goal to refrain from bringing junk fliers into his living space. By sorting through postal deliveries outside, and dropping unneeded materials directly into the trash bin, he bypasses a huge source of collecting. Canceling magazine and newspaper subscriptions is also a good move for some. For others, a worthy goal might involve avoiding thrift shops and trash bins. The ability to sit at the kitchen table to enjoy meals, or being able to lie flat in bed without heaving mounds of junk off it beforehand are worthy aims, as well.

Trouble is, the hoarder has difficulty determining what's a realistic goal and what is not. Here's where a supportive coach can come in handy.

Such a coach or helper can offer a non-judgmental perspective, along with organizational guidance. When the going gets rough, they cheerlead, keeping the hoarder on task when distractions and frustrations overwhelm. In the event that long-lost love letters or other significant materials are unearthed, they permit a brief detour, but then return the hoarder's focus to the job at hand.

Book-loving Betty's helper and childhood chum, Jim, agrees not to remove her possessions without permission. He also assists her to set guidelines as to what's okay to bring home and what's not before they begin.

For her part, Betty accepts that she will not obsess, fondle, or read any books as she sorts them. Additionally, she's only allowed to handle them once, and will not retrieve materials once dumped.

In preparation for the real thing, Betty practices decluttering via role-play during counseling sessions. Taking a dry run, she mentally categorizes books to sell, books to toss, books she plans to share, and those she wants to keep. With visualization as part of the process, she sees herself placing each book in the appropriate box; ones to keep, she envisions, she'll tidily return to her bookshelves.

When Betty's become adept at addressing these mental images, actual exposure comes next. She drops by a favorite book store, chats with the proprietor, then retreats. The following day she reenters, handles a book, puts it down, and then departs. This process is repeated until the emotional charge—her salivating lust for books—diminishes.

Anticipatory anxiety—imagining the discarding—can be far worse than the act itself, which is a big reason many never get around to doing so. It may help to know that anxiety is at its zenith at onset of discarding, but in time, as junk exits, tension and fear diminish to a large extent.

To overcome apprehension, some find stress reduction tools invaluable. Guided imagery, a gentle but powerful technique, helps one relax to positive effect. Such imagery might simply involve engaging in reverie as to how great it'll be when the trash is gone. Slightly more complex imagery may include noting how it feels to reunite with one's children.

Then there's yoga; in addition to reducing stress, it irons out physical kinks. Meditation by simply following the breath, or listening to soothing music may work for some. Progressive muscle relaxation, biofeedback, self-hypnosis, massage, and many other options exist; one might experiment a bit to find a tool that helps.

First thing each morning Tara gives herself precisely ten minutes to worry and to obsess. "Gradually," she notes with a laugh, "my need to do this has diminished, which *really* gives me something to worry about!"

Also, Tara has strategically placed numerous cheery *Post-it* notes throughout her apartment. As reminders to feel her emotions and confront her fears, they enjoin her to *Relax, Smile,* and to *Enjoy this scary moment.* While observing her thoughts and anxieties as they arise, useful information is revealed. This heightened state of self-awareness then allows her to challenge her beliefs regarding her possessions. As a result, her fear of falling ill should she fail to keep collecting shrinks to manageable proportions. If she's still overwhelmed prior to decluttering session, she ingests an anti-anxiety medication.

The Anxiety & Phobia Workbook by Edmund Bourne is a veritable encyclopedia for those suffering from anxiety and panic.[16] This book offers several positive tidbits for hoarders: notice any small, incremental changes; celebrate even the tiniest success; dine at the table that's just been cleared; go easy and forgive oneself for having such a debility. Should backsliding occur, rather than self-flagellate, jump back on track and note gains, not lapses.

"Even after clearing one's home," notes Dr. Randy Frost, "many hoarders have to always keep on top of their hoarding behavior. People *can* and *do* change and it is possible to say one is over something like this, but until we know more about what causes this, we won't know what a cure will look like."[17]

△△ △

Avoiding new acquisitions is key to ongoing success. Once hoarders have decluttered, they should strive to only bring home what's needed or what sparks joy. It helps to avoid making purchases to lift a depressed mood, and it's good to always ask: *Is this item truly necessary?* At minimum, if stuff continues to flow in, make certain objects exit in equal measure.

Occasionally, it helps to self-immunize. This practice involves, say, periodically identifying a bookstore that's tough to resist or a dumpster that beckons, and then envisioning a desirable object inside, but walking away without laying claim to it. For some, limiting the space in which to hoard—confining clutter to a spare bedroom or to a single closet—may be of use. Performing a seasonal deep cleaning that includes chucking out accumulated junk can also keep clutter from reappearing. A spousal contract, perhaps specifically limiting the amount and types of accumulation permitted, may save a rocky marriage.

Donald got rid of his car and now uses public transportation. This puts an intentional crimp in what he can tote home to objects that he can carry. Sally set up an executive hub she's dubbed the *Brain Center*. From here, she conducts all business: pays bills, writes letters, makes lists, posts notes to self, and it's where she goes to make most decisions. Her desk is organized with files labeled: *To do, To call, Bills to pay, Stuff to read*, and *Pending*. Three crates hunker adjacent: one for recycling, one for donations, the other she fills, then hefts, to a consignment shop.

Lack of desire to change is a common reason folks drown in their clutter. In fact, hoarding may persist thanks to its *secondary gains*. By this we mean that hoarding, despite its inherent problems, may be so comfortably familiar that it affords some sort of advantage, be it a release from responsibility or it allows the individual to be the focus of concern and attention, albeit negative in nature. Hoarding may also serve insofar as it causes one to miss work, particularly if it's a job one detests.

Hanging on to junk can create the illusion of the ability to hang onto the past. Furthermore, hoarding might enable one to collect disability benefits, or helps to keep others at at a distance. Additionally, the busyness involved in collecting can fill emptiness.

As an important *secondary gain:* as long as their home environment is a mess, hoarders needn't face the challenges that accompany normalcy or success. Consciously or not, the individual may figure: *Why change when my hoarding offers a convenient excuse for my unhappiness or for my lack of function?*

Like Norman, Stan hangs on to stuff for fear he'll forget crucial events. Yet, unlike Norman, he's fiercely determined to clear his living space. As he divests, he tries to be selective as to the mementos he saves. First, he tosses out items of low emotional impact such as postcards accumulated from his travels. Then he works up the gumption to discard emotion-laden items.

As he finds letters and trinkets from his deceased beloved grandmother, he asks himself, "Can I toss this broken figurine that she gave me when I was five? And if I do, does it mean I've abandoned her memory? Part of me wants to keep it all, but I also want to let go and move on, which means I'm pretty darn conflicted."

Denise Linn, author and Feng Shui expert, believes that clutter interferes with living a fulfilled life. To achieve fulfillment, she recommends taking note of the relationship one has with their stuff. This is done by taking hold of an object and asking: *How does it make me feel?*

If there's an uplift—if that item makes one feel good or if it nourishes—hang onto it. If nothing is felt, or if heaviness overwhelms, dump it. All things possessed but not enjoyed should be eighty-sixed. Anything that languishes about unused, pass it on.

Furthermore, she suggests turning inward to check one's feelings as the clutter dissipates: *Am I relaxed and more clear-headed, or am I anxious, depressed, or do I feel exposed?*[18]

Along the same vein, popular Japanese tidiness guru Marie Kondo recommends picking up each item and asking if it sparks joy. Using the emotions and not the intellect as a tool to sort, she advocates keeping only those things that inspire happiness. In doing so, she promises, one's home will become orderly and life will be joy-filled.

While most decluttering methods propose a room-by-room approach, Kondo's *KonMari Method* involves organizing by way of category. Sort and purge like items—say, all clothes, books or foodstuffs—and then remove them. Her reasoning: rather than focus on decluttering in a single locale, it's likely that similar items are scattered throughout the house. Kondo further recommends not putting anything away until everything is sorted. Then, once rid of all discardables, the individual is enjoined to designate a specific place for each category of item kept, which should make them easier to locate.[19]

Despite the immense popularity of her program, Kondo's detractors label her as highly eccentric. "We are not "detoxing" our environment as much borrowing someone else's neurosis as a form of distraction," says writer Flannery Dean with reference to Kondo's scheme.[20]

Kondo *does* manage to elevate her OCD traits and eccentricities as virtues. While anthropomorphizing her socks, she expresses concern for their "feelings." Kondo also sees family as an obstacle to the perfect lifestyle. She's such a zealous discarder that her family has barred her from purging their stuff. To circumvent their mandate, instead of ask permission, she recommends, "Don't let your family see;" a sketchy rule at best, which suggests stealth and covert removal as part and parcel to her mind-set.

Eye Movement Desensitization and Reprocessing therapy (EMDR) is a form of psychotherapy developed by Francine Shaprio, Ph. D., which holds that disturbing memories are the result of psychopathology. Discovered by accident in the late 1980s, when Shapiro experienced a disturbing thought, she noticed that her eyes moved rapidly and involuntarily. Curious about this, as she deliberately entertained more unpleasant thoughts, while bringing her eye movements under conscious control, voila...her anxiety diminished.

Moreover, she found that her distressing memories held less sway in the long-term. Her experience led her to hypothesize that traumatic events generally upset the excitatory inhibitory balance of the brain, and result in pathological changes to the nervous system. Actively engaging the brain's natural adaptive information processing mechanisms, she posited, can rebalance the brain, thereby reducing the impact of distressingly troublesome emotions.

Today, the formal version of EMDR is based on the notion that our negative thoughts, feelings, and behaviors result from unprocessed memories. The standardized EMDR procedure now involves simultaneous focus on the spontaneous associations that arise as a result of traumatic images, thoughts, emotions, as well as one's bodily sensations, while performing bilateral stimulation.

Bilateral stimulation, the core element of EMDR, most commonly involves eye movement, but can also take the form of auditory input or tactile activity that one performs in a rhythmic, side-to-side pattern. For example, visual bilateral stimulation may mean watching a hand move rhythmically, or following a moving light with one's eyes as it alternates from left to right and back again. Auditory bilateral stimulation may entail listening to tones that alternately stimulate the left and right brain hemispheres.

Such an experience prompts a cascade of changes that can initially be experienced as decreased physiological arousal or reduced tension, and ultimately lead to mental changes, such as decreased worry and distress. Amazingly, these shifts are often experienced quickly and with ease, as opposed to most therapeutic treatments that tend to be prolonged and require introspection, insight that depends upon massive overhaul of the psyche.

At inception, EMDR was controversial within the psychological community and its efficacy, as compared to other treatments, was questioned. Essentially, the simple underlying mechanism of brain rebalancing still remains subject to debate. However, EMDR is now recommended as being highly effective in cases of trauma. The American Psychiatric Association, as well as the Departments of Veterans Affairs, the International Society for Traumatic Stress Studies, and the World Health Organization tout its benefits.

Initially used to treat military veterans for post traumatic stress disorder (PTSD), EMDR attests traumatic or distressing experiences overwhelm one's normal coping skills. Furthermore, EMDR asserts that the memory and stimuli associated with the original trauma get imbedded in the nervous system and is inadequately processed.

Nowadays, EMDR has a variety of applications. It's used to treat rape victims; various forms of depression; as well as several mental health disorders. Specifically borderline personality and bipolar illness; as well as a variety of compulsive disorders, including phobias; along with body dysmorphia, where a person falsely believes something is wrong with their appearance, can be relieved with this simple, effective intervention. Also, it's effective in treatment of phantom limb pain.

Similar to cognitive behavioral therapy (CBT), EMDR aims to reduce distress and to strengthen adaptive beliefs related to traumatic events. Unlike CBT, however, EMDR doesn't involve a detailed review with regard to the triggering incident, nor does it require the challenging of beliefs, or the necessity to re-expose oneself to scary circumstances.

The use of EMDR in instances of hoarding holds that excessive acquisition and cluttering embed in the psyche as a result of unprocessed trauma. Specific protocols for working with clients who hoard are detailed in the book *Eye Movement*

Desensitization and Reprocessing Therapy Scripted Protocols and Summary Sheets: Treating Anxiety, Obsessive-Compulsive, and Mood-Related Conditions.[21]

While many practitioners use EMDR to treat hoarding, the authors know of no research that specifically targets its use in this regard. Given that most hoarders have taken years to acquiesce to treatment, and while EMDR may have a rapid, positive impact on the client's behavior and cognition, the complete decluttering of the environment requires time and patience.

⌂⌂ ⌂

Akin to loss of an old friend, one may actually grieve curtailment of hoarding behaviors. The hoarder's identity—the collecting, the time spent obsessing, even the inconvenience and harassment of others—all that which so thoroughly defines them, is bundled into their mindset. Cease to collect, and one must mourn all the years lost to obsession. Cease to collect and awareness of loss—of relationships and of opportunities—come into focus.

While decluttering can release the grip of hoarding, recovery is never done. With no ultimate cure, and for tidiness to last, self-monitoring must be lifelong. This is where long-term therapy or a support group can be invaluable.

Sam's newfound belief in God helps him discard and keep a tidy house. "God, I realize, provides for my needs, so I no longer need to save everything."

Buffered by this trust, he's able to toss out a dozen crates of aluminum foil; each case holds fifty rolls. Should he need more, he figures, he'll just purchase them. This new attitude is a refreshing, far cry from his fearful, angst-driven persona of old.

CHAPTER 9

Light at Dumpster's Bottom—Communities and Neighbors Interface with Hoarders

*"Good works are links that form a chain of love.
In this life we cannot do great things.
We can only do small things with great love."*

— MOTHER TERESA

JANICE'S PREDECESSOR, ALSO A REGISTERED nurse, went out on a crisis call to visit an elderly woman, we'll call Desiree. Having thoroughly filled up her home, Desiree resided within the trash pile in her driveway. When the nurse arrived to check on her, the older woman crawled out from the junk pile and loaded on the charm.

Proven so delightfully compelling, she managed to convince the worker as to her competence so no intervention seemed indicated.

Weeks later, following a neighbor's concerned tip, this same crisis worker paid Desiree a return visit. As before, the affable woman chatted away.

As the visit went swimmingly, Desiree happened to mention that her back and buttocks pained her, so the nurse requested a peek.

Initially, Desiree resisted, but then obliged. Peeling of her putrid shirt that stuck to inflamed, scabby flesh revealed festering sores, a-squirm with maggots.

Trying not to gag, the crisis nurse offered her a trip to the hospital.

"It's notta problem," Desiree insisted, "and thank you very much, but I don't want or need medical care!"

Citing a danger to self and grave disability, the worker wrote out an involuntary hold, and then paramedics arrived to scoop Desiree up and away for treatment.

Given the sparse information garnered prior to the first visit, Desiree was perfectly entitled to continue living in her driveway trash, which meant the law could not intervene. In light of the newer concerns regarding her medical status, coupled with her denial of the problem, everything shifted.

The law protects the rights of individuals to a point, which includes abiding by their prerogative to make terrible decisions. Yet, when it became clear that Desiree posed an imminent risk to herself, she lost the right to self-determination, which then allowed the County to take charge.

"They've singled me out for harassment and have unfair expectations!" is eighty-one-year-old Myra's usual refrain when the annual inspection of her apartment comes around.

Myra is a seasoned veteran of these evaluations, yet only the threat of eviction propels her to make her apartment livable. After weathering over sixteen years of near-evictions, these brushes have taken a toll on Myra's health. Insisting that management has it in for her, she's unwilling or incapable of acknowledging the extreme filth and clutter of her living conditions. As a result, she suffers from asthma, migraines, panic attacks, and has multiple allergies. While past referrals for medical care, and for therapy, as well as access to anxiety-reducing medication go unrequited, Myra continues to lament: *Nobody's helping, and no one cares!*

Folks who chronically refuse assistance, despite many offers to help, all while complaining about lack of support, are what's known as *Help-Rejecting Complainers*. Their habit of blaming others, as hoarders often do, negates any possible improvement or change.

△△ △

Most neighborhoods have their Myra; a notorious individual whose trash house or apartment blights their environs. In such instances, a draped landscape of blue tarpaulins, often stretched to cover stacks of junk, doesn't indicate the presence of a trendy megalithic Cristo installation. Beneath those tarps lurk tens of thousands of papers and magazines, stacked or tossed alongside dismembered appliances, and auto parts. Myriad other unidentifiable objects are also cast throughout the weeds and foliage, creating a veritable junk garden.

Such a scene brings us to Judith, a former librarian who lives in a tidy, fashionable neighborhood. The eerie sight of her front yard heaped high with books brings to mind an imminent book-burning.

"I've even thought about moving because this is *so* ridiculous," sighs Celia, a neighbor with an unobstructed view of Judith's property. "Obviously, that place is a hazard for her, too."

One day, the police arrive and make their way past pyramids of rotting books—an attractant to rats and rodents, which happens to violate County Code—to serve a warrant, then they enter Judith's abode.

Inside, rat corpses are strewn about. Human feces splatter the bathrooms and food-smears encrust countertops, as well. Water stagnates in the backyard swimming pool, which invites the proliferation of mosquitoes. As a result of the hazards, Judith is cited for violating health and safety standards.

Agreeably and surprisingly, she swiftly clears the mess. Yet she promptly resumes dumping books and garbage in her yard again. Round-and-round Judith, the County, and her neighbors spin, until over a decade later a court-ordered psychiatric evaluation is finally mandated.

Grudgingly, Judith obliges to an assessment, whereupon, she is deemed fascinatingly articulate, and highly intelligent. Most relevant, she's considered to be competent, so therapy and a medical evaluation can only be recommended, not required. So naturally, she declines.

In the County where Judith lives, law enforcement, fire, public health, the building department, APS, and mental health agencies often band together to persuade, and if need be, force intractable hoarders to clean up their messes. To that end, a neglected property ordinance, jokingly referred to as the *Ozzie and Harriet Law,* helps regulate the outdoor storage of belongings.

When a complaint is filed, offenders have ten days to remove their junk or to reply as to why they cannot comply. In the event that they fail to convince, or remain uncooperative, the County hires a contractor to haul their trash away. As an unfortunate side effect, homeless rats scamper onto adjacent properties.

As with any law, there are loopholes; this one merely addresses debris in front and side yards. This means the offender can shift treasures to the backyard, where the festering impact remains covert.

On a related note, hoarders with a penchant for cars park them, willy-nilly, in their yards. In response, many cities and counties prohibit parking on lawns or on unpaved spaces, including the storing of vehicles on private property. Additionally, they often deem boat or trailer storage in non-prescribed places to be a violation of zoning code. For control purposes, some communities also have vehicle abatement programs, making it a no-no to abandon cars on public streets.

The Municipal Code in San Jose, California, for instance, further enumerates minimum acceptable cosmetic standards for residential dwellings. Regulatory standards include the number of structures allowed, what kind of items may be stored, and where that exterior storage can be placed. Furthermore, it specifies precisely what stored materials and circumstances cause blight to prevent neighboring properties from becoming devalued.

To that end, these junked-up properties are scrutinized with an eye to the presence of the following: discarded furniture; car parts, appliances, and debris in the yard; doorways that are obstructed; a lack of a building's structural safety; the presence of wastewater or toxic chemicals; the existence of fire hazards, such as overgrown vegetation and dry grasses; unfenced swimming pools; as well as the presence of rodents and of certain winged insects. To educate the public, this city offers a pertinent flier, *What About Packrats and Garbage Residences?*

When someone complains—typically when debris has expanded into public view—authorities swiftly intervene. Occupants and/or property owners are then informed of the violation in writing, which also includes a stated deadline in which to achieve compliance. The recalcitrant resident ends up being fined with stiff penalties—as much as $2500 a day—for failure to cooperate.

Ignore the warning and the City takes legal measures that culminate in hiring a contractor to haul the debris away, and the owner is charged with the cost of cleanup. Should fees go unpaid, a lien is placed against the property and collected upon sale.

Hoarders who perpetually inflict unsafe conditions on themselves and their neighborhood may be referred to the District Attorney for criminal prosecution. In extreme cases—those that pose imminent danger—the hoarder is forcibly removed.

"The challenge, as our population ages," notes former Santa Cruz County Mental Health Services Director Rama Khalsa, "and as elderly people want to stay in their homes, is how we as a society can support the decision to remove them. Frequently, if folks have family, we don't get involved. But if there's no family or if they're estranged, then it falls to [county agencies and law enforcement] who at least assess the situation."[1]

Indeed, as Baby Boomers age, increasing numbers find themselves alone, overwhelmed, and unable to cope. As a result, communities marshal their resources and spend thousands of dollars on their worst cases. Yet, help is often needed long before the situation becomes dire.

Yet, as a reminder, these packrats have the right to live as they wish, so long as they don't interfere with the rights of others. But precisely what constitutes an interfering hazard? Is it that unsightly paint job, or the presence of too many cars, or the storing of combustibles that might ignite and entire neighborhood?

By encouraging residents to report each other for code violations, Santa Ana, California takes clean-up to the level of *1984*-style science fiction. Enjoined to tattle on others for broken windows, and for structurally unsound fences, or for the presence of "improper" balcony or patio storage creates a dandy breeding ground for resentment. Their list of reportables include: stagnant pools of water, the storing of construction materials, wrongful parking of autos, strewn auto parts, and unpainted buildings. But wait, there's more: dish antennas visible from the street or placed where they can be seen by surrounding properties are deemed offensive, and therefore reportable. Staging a garage sale on a weekday also constitutes a violation.

△△ △

Arlington County, Virginia is home to a far more enlightened *Hoarding Task Force*. When problems arise, its pre-guardianship panel, comprised of citizens and several county representatives, consults with APS to determine if intervention is warranted. In this process, each case is carefully examined, using Dr. Barbara Soniat's *Capacity-Risk Model* to evaluate the hoarder's level of function. This tool assesses the capacity to perform self-care, taking into consideration the individual's psychological status, their financial resources, along with their ability to manage funds, and their existing social supports.

If an individual is deemed functional—meaning the hoarder can handle his or her basic needs—the right to self-determination is respected. If the capacity to perform self-care is moderate and the person's level of risk is also moderate, support is set in place to avert any crisis that might arise. Should the ability to handle basic needs be assessed as poor and if the individual's safety is at risk, staff mobilizes to place the person under guardianship and may possibly impose a move to safe housing.

APS is mandated to investigate cases of abuse and neglect, even when that neglect is self-inflicted. Commonly, APS staff assesses the home for potentially hazardous conditions and intervenes when indicated. As a result, they come in contact with many hoarders.

Should the hoarder be receptive, they are referred to services such as Meals on Wheels, In-Home Support, or to a senior outreach program, which helps with home repairs or tax preparation. Should more assistance be needed, they recommend a payeeship to manage finances and pay bills or possibly even a conservatorship.

Referrals to APS frequently come from animal protection services, as well as from other public agencies. Family and friends, or neighbors also make referrals. Neighbors tend to avoid grousing out of a desire to coexist or fear of retaliation, but when at wit's end they end up filing a complaint.

In one California county, a neighbor contacted public health about the unbearable stench emanating from the hoarder's home adjacent. "We're afraid to open our doors, because rats run into our house from the rubble next door." This situation was reported, then evaluated and declared a public nuisance.

On occasion, a property is subject to summary abatement, meaning the nuisance is so dire that it must be removed post-haste, bypassing the usual judicial proceedings. Cause for abatement includes the presence of open sewage, or hazardous waste, or the presence of toxic materials. An abandoned refrigerator with the door still attached creates an attractive danger for children to crawl into, then shut the door and suffocate, so appliances as this also require immediate removal.

Forced cleanup can be the result of criminal charges, and mandated re-checks at designated intervals may be a part of the hoarder's legal sentence. Occasionally, psychiatric counseling or medications may also be required.

During Janice's tenure as mental health crisis nurse, she wrote the occasional 5150. A 5150, as defined by the California Welfare and Institutions Code—also known as a *seventy-two-hour hold*, or an *involuntary detention*, or simply a *Hold*—allows police and designated mental health professionals to take a person into custody if that individual poses a risk to self, or to others due to a mental disorder or to alcoholism.

Never a decision lightly made, a valid 5150 requires that the subject pose an *imminent* danger to him or herself or to others or that they are gravely disabled, specifically, that they're incapable of providing food, clothing or shelter for themselves. By <u>imminent,</u> we mean the danger can not be intuited as something that will occur in the future; the danger must be immediate, Those who meet the criteria for a 5150 can be forcibly removed from their homes.

As imagined, imposing hospitalization against one's will rarely makes for smooth-sailing, so police are often involved. After a thorough medical evaluation, which usually takes place in an emergency room, psychiatric hospitalization is typically the end result.

Defying logic, when the hoarder is removed from their messy home, they often present as quite coherent, with little-to-no evidence of psychosis or even a slight hint as to their wretched living conditions. Usually, these people resist treatment and minimize their living situation.

Should the hospital fail to probe, or if concrete evidence in the form of photos or video are lacking, hospital staff may wonder why the fuss, and swiftly release the offender. As a result, the hoarder who managed to pass for "normal" returns home, alienated and more mistrustful than ever, to then resume their problematic behaviors.

Here's where photos of the house, inside and out, are worth a thousand words. To that end, the prescient outreach worker does well to carry a camera or camera-capable cell phone in the field to document the visuals. Inevitably, hospital staff will find such information sobering, which can then buy more time for treatment.

In truth, psychiatric hospitals are ill-equipped to deal with the hoarder's unique problem-set. Given the 72-hour limit, cognitive-behavior therapy cannot be swiftly implemented, so in the best case, the hoarder benefits from medication and accepts aftercare referrals.

While detained, the hoarder faces legal certification procedures that mostly involve assessment of competence. In California, this process occasionally culminates in a Lanterman Petris Short (LPS) Conservatorship, which gives a specific agency, commonly the County's Public Guardian, authority to treat and place the incompetent individual without their consent.

Initially, the LPS Conservatorship was crafted to end reckless, inappropriate, indefinite, and involuntary commitment of the mentally ill. These days, this law also includes those who are gravely disabled by virtue of dementia or developmental disability, along with those impaired by severe alcoholism. When implemented, the LPS Conservatorship allows the hoarder to be removed from circulation and then placed in a controlled living situation, which prevents collection of more junk.

LPS law, serving as the most extreme legal means of non-criminal containment, is applied to the hoarder whose activities interfere with the health and welfare of others or when the hoarder's life is in danger. Given that two, seemingly conflicting goals are at play—safeguarding the rights of the individual while also protecting public safety—at every turn, the rights of the individual in question are paramount. For instance, the hoarder has the right to appeal each step in the certification process and legal counsel must be offered.

Remember Doris, with all those dead cats? She got LPS Conserved, then placed in a locked facility, where—her desire for more cats notwithstanding—she actually found contentment. Norman, who scrounged through dumpsters in search of McDonald's Happy Meal Boxes, was also conserved, which gave the County the right to toss out his trash, and thereby maintain him in stable housing.

According to California law, property owners have the right to peacefully co-exist alongside their neighbors. So when hoarders fill their yards with trash, creating a public nuisance, they can be sued for causing emotional distress. To that end, whole communities have been known to organize to sue their neighboring hoarder. On the other hand, concerned neighbors also stage clean-up parties, hire contractors to haul away messes, and cut down overgrown brush to help the individual at their own expense.

In one instance, after initially going along with the support offered, the hoarder abruptly refused her neighbor's efforts, so the group obtained a court order. When Environmental Health and Building Code enforcement showed up, the woman barred the door, which prompted further legal sanctions. Forced inspection of home and yard, then revealed multiple structural problems, as well as health hazards. The end result mandated that she make regular psychiatric visits, and that she hire ongoing help to keep the property clean.

Alas, as soon as probation ended, this woman began to collect all over again. The yard and house quickly filled up, causing rats and flies to return. So once more, the neighbors sought help, and an LPS Conservatorship posed the ultimate recourse.

One elderly Florida couple's attempts to sell their property were repeatedly stymied by the garbage dump situated on the other side of their fence. After three years trying, they gave up, moved out, and rented elsewhere. With their own home unmarketable and un-rentable, they had to leave it vacant.

When homes are sold, some states require full disclosure as to the property's historical status. This means divulging the existence of a public nuisance, including a trash house, even when it's situated several doors down. Should this tidbit come to light, it can void the sale, and the buyer can also sue if this information remains undisclosed.

Not all communities and neighbors are at odds. Orange County in California averts potential trash build-up by assisting the elderly to cart out their accumulated garbage. They also help cut overgrown brush and repair broken windows. Another subgroup of that community assists their neighboring hoarder by removing accumulated junk on a monthly basis, while another bunch foots the bill for garbage pick-up on behalf of a woman who can't afford it.

Clearly, such acts aren't entirely altruistic. Neighbors in Huntington Beach, California banned together to force college professor Elena Zagustin to clean up her property or to move out. Spanning a decade they'd repeatedly requested she remove yard junk and bring her property up to minimum standards; they even volunteered to help with cleanup and to maintain her yard. Zagustin rejected all offers, ignored several court orders to tidy up the property up, and eventually did jail time.

At one point, subsequent to the group's futile calls to local agencies asking that they intervene, they took Zagustin to Small Claims Court. This Court limits the amount of reparations allowed per claimant; depending on the county, these numbers range from $3000 to $5000. While that sum may not seem like much, when twenty-or-so folks ban together, as happened with Zagustin, a liability claim of $100,000 can amass.[2]

Since personal taste can span a broad spectrum, what constitutes an eyesore for one may be a thing of beauty to another. Therefore, it's incumbent upon the judge assigned to Small Claims cases to determine if a perceived "fault" is merely a matter of taste, and to also ascertain if claimants are motivated by vengeance.

Occasionally, a case can involve a counter-lawsuit invoked by the hoarder for infringement of the right to peaceful enjoy their domicile. One brilliant,

My Husband's Under Here Somewhere

retired professor—a specialist hoarder, if you will—kept gallon-size, urine-filled bottles that crowded her living room. When she suffered a fall, paramedics got quite the eyeful and as a result, she was placed on an involuntary hold. Upon removal from her peculiarly appointed home, she was so incensed that she sued the county for infringement of her rights.

At times, matters escalate out of control and require the marshaling of many resources, along with the expertise of multiple community agencies. Janice describes her county's own version of *The War Room,* where county officials representing nearly a dozen agencies assemble to problem-solve regarding their most complex, recalcitrant hoarders. Their particular group includes: APS; the Public Guardian, which acts on behalf of incompetent, incapacitated persons; Mental Health; Public Health; the Planning and Health Departments; as well as police and fire agencies.

This time, they gather to strategize how best to deal with an elderly hermit. For years, Jonah Sloane, an alcoholic, has lived in abject squalor. As a result, his home is a firetrap that poses serious concern to neighbors on his hillside street. Further complicating matters, he threatens to shoot anyone trying to intervene.

Recently, Jonah's mattress ignited, and as the fire department doused the flames, they took note of his living conditions. "This time we got lucky," says the Fire Marshall, "but there was so much stuff jammed in the way that we had trouble entering. If another fire got going, we'd be hard-pressed to get in fast enough to put it out. At any rate, we found the resident on his mattress bleeding heavily and called the paramedics."

"Also, he has a cache of shotguns; there's a weapon stashed behind each door. Fortunately, we took photos."

As pictures are passed, the Marshall points out Jonah's blood-soaked mattress and the blood-spattered floors and walls. With blood no longer able to clot, terminal hemorrhage is a common occurrence for end-stage alcoholics.

"We managed to cajole Mr. Sloane to visit the hospital, where he was diagnosed with pneumonia, congestive heart failure, and a bleeding disorder secondary to drink. But he then refused treatment and returned home."

Hence, the reason that the group convened.

At this point, Diane, case manager with APS, who knows Jonah best, speaks up, "You need to understand that Jonah views government as the enemy. So believe me," she cautions, "since his home is all he's got, if he's strong enough, he'll use his weapons to fight us to the bitter end.

"Last week," she continues, "Dr. Griffin and I went I went out to do an assessment. The police went, too, as a precaution. The night prior, Jonah stood in the street screaming and raving, so neighbors called it in. When we talked outside—he's never let me in the house—he seemed weak and short of breath, so I offered to take him to the hospital, but he refused."

"At the time, he didn't seem ill enough, or out control to the extent that we could force him to go. But I think he'll die, or set the neighborhood on fire, or shoot someone, if we don't intervene soon."

The room went silent as attendees pondered the weight of this remark.

"Surely, no one in their right mind chooses to live as this man does," the Planning Department Supervisor jumps in. "I want to know why mental health doesn't just hospitalize him?"

"Yeah, obviously something's wrong," chimes the Director of Environmental Health, "so why can't mental health force the man into treatment?"

"Well, why doesn't Environmental Health get out there to inspect for health hazards," queries a second APS worker.

"The Planning Department should slap a red-tag on that unsafe structure," blurts a Public Guardian staffer.

The room erupts. Tempers flare, as fingers are pointed, with agency staff busily blaming each other for failing to act.

"True, hoarding and cluttering can be symptoms of mental illness," Diane interjects, "but it can also be a lifestyle choice. So until the situation poses an immediate hazard, as most everyone here knows, this man has the right to make bad decisions."

△△ △

Bringing the group back on task, Dr. Griffin describes last week's scene: "The place was a mess. The weed-choked yard was strewn with trash drifts. Some piles, stacked against the exterior walls of the house, reached the roof. We knocked several minutes, then tried windows and the other doors. Finally, after a bit of a wait, Jonah emerged.

"Wearing filthy clothes that smelt of urine and feces, he was scarecrow-thin," Dr. Griffin remarks with a grimace. "Greatly resenting our presence, he came across as tense, angry and defiant. Conscious of the potential for violence, we kept our distance.

"In the past, the law rested on Jonah's side. Never before, to our knowledge, has he come across as an imminent danger to himself or to others. Guns and fire hazards notwithstanding, given the man's frail state—his bleeding in particular—his health appears to be in jeopardy, which makes him a potential risk to himself.

"As I did my usual probing," the doctor continues, "Jonah told us he lives off a small pension, has been a recluse most of his life, is furious with the County for interfering, and wants to be left alone. He has no family, except a second cousin, but they ceased contact long ago.

"Previously, he lost two other properties due to unpaid taxes. Two years back, the County forced him to clear the debris surrounding his house, a matter that he feels is nobody's business.

"He says he has guns." Dr. Griffin pauses to examine his notes, then resumes, "but he claims not to have bullets. Yes, he has a sufficient supply of food; a neighbor drives him to the market. He says he has running water and viable plumbing. And by his own statement, he isn't suicidal.

"Overall, I found him to be paranoid, irritable, and in very poor physical condition. He's also an intelligent, rather lucid, interesting fellow. When we offered access to medical care, he refused and terminated the interview. However," Dr. Griffin ponders a bit, then sums up, "given his failing health, as documented by his recent hemorrhage, along with those photos, the man poses a sufficient risk to himself. So I recommend we proceed as swiftly as possible filing papers for a probate conservatorship. It'll be tricky to serve them, utmost care must be taken in this regard."

Police Officer Chet Morgan takes the floor. "Okay, everyone listen up. We know this man has weapons, so when the Public Guardian presents him with papers, law enforcement and the paramedics will stand by to ensure a safe transition. To do this, we'll place an officer at each external door.

"First off, Dave...," he addresses a fellow policeman, "you get his attention on the bullhorn, let him know we're coming in, then...we rush him. Don't give him time to prepare, just go. We don't want anyone hurt."

The group fine-tunes the plan, trying to cover all contingencies. APS will take the lead and coordinate with the other agencies. Dr. Griffin will quickly complete probate conservatorship papers and then the Public Guardian will petition the court for the legal authority to intervene. Once this happens, whether Jonah agrees or not, he will be taken to the hospital for medical treatment. Legal counsel for the County blesses this plan.

As soon as he's removed, Environmental Health agrees to secure a warrant in order to inspect the home for safety hazards. Police and Fire Departments promise to make themselves available to soothe and educate neighbors. "I just hope Jonah survives for a time," notes the APS staffer, "so he can reap the benefits of our endeavor."

⌂⌂ ⌂

Clearly, there's no cookie-cutter answer on how to deal with the non-compliant hoarder. As with Jonah, this multi-faceted issue involves tremendous community resources and can be harrowing to resolve. When the issue is this complex, counties achieve the optimal end result through mutual cooperation rather than finger pointing.

The first order of business in Jonah's case was to secure a probate conservatorship. The probate conservatorship is less restrictive than an LPS Conservatorship. When a person is unable to care for himself, this conservatorship is authorized by a judge who appoints a *conservator* to be responsible for the care of the designated individual, also known as the *conservatee*.

There are two parts to a probate; the conservatorship of *the person*, and the conservatorship of *the estate*. Conservatorship of *the person* bestows responsibility for care and protection onto the conservator, whereas conservatorship of *the estate* assigns a conservator to handle the person's finances. The same person may be appointed to fulfill one or both of these functions. Sometimes family or a friend acts as conservator of the person, whereas the Public Guardian may be appointed conservator of the estate, or vise-versa. On occasion, one or both of these forms of conservatorship may be indicated.

Should a relative or friend offer to serve in either capacity, they're carefully scrutinized with an eye to their intentions and as to their capacity to perform the required supportive functions. Given that fiduciary and physical or emotional abuse of the elderly are rampant, it's critical to ascertain the potential conservator's true agenda.

If the hoarder wishes to fight a probate conservatorship, as is their right, an attorney is appointed and a court date is set. During court, dysfunction in the form of grave disability—specifically, the inability to provide food, clothing, and shelter—must be proven. Once again, this is where photos are of huge benefit, particularly when the hoarder comes across as perfectly normal. Should the bid for conservatorship fail to pass muster, the hoarder is free to resume their previous lifestyle.

Should the hoarder lose their case, the appointed guardian assumes responsibility. This may involve securing an unsafe home, hiring help to clean it out, and if necessary, selling the place to pay for care and placement. This form of conservatorship is then subject to annual review and the conservatee has the right to appeal each time.

Unlike an LPS Conservatorship, probate conservatorship doesn't automatically include the authority to medicate persons against their will, or force the conservatee to be kept in a locked setting. Such powers must be specifically requested. In Jonah's case, the probate conservatorship stipulated that medical care be provided against his wishes and that he be detained until stabilized.

Agonized screams brought another female hoarder to the County's attention. Previously diagnosed with sepsis secondary to breast cancer, the woman steadfastly refused all medical attention.

Yet when her very vocal anguish kept neighbors up all hours, a probate conservatorship was quickly established, granting the Public Guardian authority to hospitalize and treat her. Against her protestations, surgery to drain and stabilize the massive tumor and infection, along with forced pain medications, and follow-up care were provided. Thankfully, her health improved to the extent that she could enjoy several pain-free, tolerable final months.

⌂⌂ ⌂

So how do other agencies interface with the hoarder and with each other?

Agency referrals, neighbor's complaints, and incidents of hoarder's antisocial behaviors bring law enforcement into the picture. When police arrive on the scene and determine if *probable cause* exists, meaning if resident is violating the law or poses a danger to self or to others, the authorities can enter the abode without a search warrant to perform a "welfare check."

Typically, before entry the police knock, await a response, announce themselves, and if there's no reply, enter the premises uninvited. Occasionally, the owner or tenant is unwilling or unable to respond due to incapacity, and may need life-saving assistance.

When psychosis or dangerous behaviors are evident, mental health is contacted for evaluation and possible intervention. Given that services can only be provided to those who voluntarily accept it, until a crisis occurs, mental healthstaff cannot intervene. Often, this means looking to neighbors, friends, or family to keep tabs on the hoarder and notify mental health when matters deteriorate. At that point, designated mental health staff can conserve or hospitalize the person against their will, or better yet, the individual is ready to accept help.

With an eye to removing or mitigating hazards involving flammable materials, Fire Departments work hand-in-hand with law enforcement. As previously noted, such hazards include tall weeds and overgrown brush, as well as junked-up yards, combustible stored materials, and improper electrical wiring. Other concerns include papers stacked near or atop heat sources or trash that's tossed into an open fireplace, then lit, sending flaming debris to waft, willy-nilly. Dropped cigarette embers are equally hazardous.

Many communities offer In-Home Supportive Services, (IHSS) which assists the elderly and disabled to remain in their homes as they lose capacity to care for themselves. Eligibility for IHSS is limited to those of low-income and includes shopping, cooking, bathing, housekeeping, and non-medical personal care. Furthermore, clutterers who receive IHSS services and are at risk of eviction can access junk removal and cleanup services. Regrettably, Jonah would have benefited from such help, but was too paranoid to accept it.

⌂⌂ ⌂

When neighbors complained about the weed encroachment on Doris' (The Pied Piper of Cats) property, they also mentioned the sewage that overflowed onto the street, yet so much more was found. A burgeoning rat infestation spilt over to other yards, and dying and dead cats were strewn about. The house itself was an eyesore of broken windows, and sported a gaping hole in the roof. Additionally, squatters camped in the carport, warming themselves over uncontained fires. As a result, the County subjected her property to abatement.

The Fire Department insisted that her weeds be cut; Environmental Health oversaw trash removal and repair of the sewage leak; and County Planning red-tagged the illegally built carport, demanding that it be deconstructed. Furthermore, the SPCA advised that all cats be treated for a contagious eye infection; if left uncared for, this highly lethal infection promised to impact the entire neighborhood.

Feisty Doris demanded a court trial. In such instances, the offender appears before a Hearing Board or in some communities, before the Board of Supervisors, to present evidence as to why abatement should not proceed. Doris, however, was a no-show for her appointed date, so her house got red-tagged and she was slapped with further fees and fines.

Red-tagging notifies the owner as to code violations, which are then recorded on the property's title and remain there until compliance is achieved. If a violation or nuisance isn't remedied in a timely manner, another letter is served, notifying the homeowner that the County will handle the issue. This missive also demands the payment of any abatement fees incurred. If the matter still goes unresolved, further fines and fees get tacked onto property taxes.

County staff doesn't perform actual clean up, but contracts with a private agency for their services instead. Typically, abatement is costly and hoarders tend to be repeat offenders. So if fees are left unpaid, fines and the cost of abatement steadily stack up with each violation.

If property taxes go delinquent, as in Jonah's case, the homeowner faces additional penalties, and possible sale of the property for outstanding taxes. Upon the property's sale, the lien is resolved after the county recoups all their incurred expenses.

When foreclosure occurs, the court may appoint a "receiver" who holds the land and its contents while legal action is pending. During this interval, the defendant has the opportunity to remedy the problem by coming up with money to clear the foreclosure.

⌂⌂ ⌂

A week after the aforementioned meeting about Jonah Sloane, conservatorship papers were complete. So APS, along with police and paramedics, returned to the scene.

After calling and knocking with no response, the police entered the house. As they carefully, cautiously moved about, loaded rifles and guns were found (So much for not having bullets!).

Located on his bedroom mattress bleeding and barely conscious, an unresistant Jonah was swiftly taken to the hospital. There, he was diagnosed with lung cancer, heart failure, and a GI bleed, and succumbed shortly thereafter.

The next meeting of the County Hoarder Task Force was exceedingly somber. Despite efforts to comfort themselves that they'd done the best they possibly could, lingering doubts remained.

Could we have acted sooner, saving Jonah pain, distress, and possibly his life? If we had intervened when he was energetic and feisty, could he have killed or harmed another? And, *Did we fail the neighbors by not responding faster?*

With no clear answers, the group *did* resolve to be more proactive. As a result, they agreed to monthly meetings to review at-risk cases and to intervene more swiftly. In the future, they proceeded to launch well-coordinated team efforts and established countywide protocols to deal with complex cases.

There's a renaissance among Community Mental Health Associations as they seek to reduce clutter-related evictions by educating landlords regarding hoarding behaviors. Additionally, such organizations try to spread the word that hoarding is, indeed, a bonafide mental illness, not merely eccentric stubbornness.

San Jose, California's Alliance for Community Care has a model program that offers case management to hoarders, as well as vocational assessment and training, and even has supportive housing. Naturally, the common obstacle to access is the hoarder's unwillingness to make use of such help.

Bill Hersh, director of another association in San Francisco, notes that five to fifteen percent of those who live in affordable housing for the disabled manifest some degree of hoarding behaviors.[3] While the Americans with Disabilities Act (ADA) prevents discrimination against disabled individuals, and despite the fact that hoarders fall into this category, many aren't protected by ADA provisions because their frequent violations of health and safety codes supersede the Disability Act. The law, *does* allow hoarders a reasonable interval to clean up their clutter.

Each year Myra, whom we've mentioned, takes full advantage of this right by repeatedly finagling apartment inspection extensions that drag on for months. As soon as she tidies up and meets minimal standards, the pressure lifts, so she invariably slumps back to accumulating again. After many years of this repeated cycle, her landlord has wised up to add ongoing contingencies, including quarterly spot checks and an increase of her damage deposit.

When intervention radically alters the hoarder's life—be it through conservatorship, psychiatric or medical hospitalization, or placement in a locked facility—outcomes vary greatly. One elderly diabetic was extracted from her trash-filled home, only to expire hours later in the emergency room. Then there are the lively siblings who were forcibly removed from their residence and now live, quite content, in a board and care facility. The brother enjoys a new set of teeth and attends junior college, whereas the sister has taken up knitting and adores playing bingo.

⌂⌂ ⌂

After much hullabaloo, the woman for whom this book is titled got LPS conserved, then went to live on the property of a sympathetic friend, until he had enough and gave her the boot. Here's Janice's version as to how that story played out:

"Inside the front door lay a dead cat being gnawed by rats," recounts Janice. "Gingerly, I stepped round it, held my breath against the stench, and got my bearings. Trash reached the ceiling and was crammed in so tight, there were none of the usual "goat trails" necessary to move about.

"Despite vast education and impressive credentials, the owners, both retired Lockheed engineers, lived in the most god-awful squalor I've ever seen. And, believe me, I've witnessed top-notch filth and wretched conditions!

"Years on end, neighbors complained to the County about the stink emanating from the house and of the rodents scurrying from the debris into their homes. Yet the couple retained a savvy lawyer who supplied them with the legal means to perpetuate their scary, unsafe lifestyle. On and on their disruptive behaviors went, until a series of fateful events.

"Some time ago," Janice continues, "the husband, a heavy drinker, extracted himself from their thoroughly unlivable house to reside in a trailer on the property. Claiming to miss his wife, he recently moved back in with her. Then, three days ago, he went missing.

"Unable to find him, the wife, who is the hoarder, certain he'd taken a tumble into the rubble, gave us a call. So there I was, accompanying police, paramedics, and the fire department. To pass from one room to another, we had to slither along on our bellies with barely a foot's gap from the ceiling. Heads tucked to avoid rafter beams, moving atop mountains of newspapers, magazines, and junk, it felt utterly surreal as we called out, searching.

"Smelling rot, mildew, mold, and dead animals, I feared I'd fall through and not be able to clamber out again. Worse yet, I feared I might *actually* find the man. As luck had it, we found no trace of him."

Two days later, an awful stench led a police dog to the body entombed within a mountain of debris. The wife, a brilliant, complicated soul met the loss with rage, then grief.

CHAPTER 10

Till Trash do Us Part— Living with or Without Your Beloved Hoarder

---

When I'm dying, someone else's life will pass before my eyes

—The Perfect Co-Dependent, Anonymous

ACTING ON A NEIGHBOR'S TIP, police arrived to check out a home in San Francisco, California. When inside, they deemed it the worst incident of hoarding they'd ever seen. Come upon a mummified body, it seems the 65 year old homeowner, unable to part with the corpse of her deceased mother, simply held onto it as she steadily filled her home with junk. Foul play wasn't suspected.[1]

As we know, the turmoil, stress, and distress caused by hoarding wreaks havoc upon all players. Unlike other OCD disorders that can be hidden, hoarding by its very nature, is so overt, so all-encompassing, that it's impossible to overlook.

Commonly, the clutter angers or bewilders other household members. It particularly rankles when requests that the hoarder cease to collect and remove their aggregation go ignored or are responded to with indignation or flimsy excuses. If the hoarder orders others to keep hands off, the occasional brave soul will defiantly tackle the mess. Should this happen, the packrat turns furious, and rather than appreciate any new-found space, they merely resume collecting.

As piles burgeon, so too does emotional distance, as well as frustration and resentment. To further heighten tension, if the hoarder is a compulsive shopper, spending sprees can spiral into financial ruin. So inevitably, hoarding strains the most loving of relationships, making it tough for the non-hoarder to honor their marriage vows.

⌂⌂ ⌂

Although married 35 years, Mattie's laid-back husband, Daniel, still finds his wife's hoarding repugnant. Even though he claims that he doesn't blame her, Mattie fires back that he's actually quite intolerant, which then prompts her attempts to spare him by hiding her activities. Yet her secretiveness annoys him all the more. Inexplicably and amazingly, Daniel still says he adores her!

"Often, my wife says she's cleared things out," sighs yet another exasperated spouse as he discusses the matter with Janice, "but nothing ever changes. Heck, I'm ready to rent a truck and haul it all away." This fellow maintains a separate bedroom and keeps that door locked. "If I don't do this, quick as a blink, my room fills with junk. Our daughter, too, locks her bedroom. Poor kid, I'm really sorry she hasta live like this."

"My wife," he continues, "can't see that we live in a war-zone and doesn't truly give a darn about the impact that all the...excuse me—crap—has on us. Yet she views absolutely everything, probably even the dust, as hugely important."

Huffily, the wife who stands nearby retorts, "Have I ever lost track of anything important? Haven't the bills always been paid on time? How I choose to live is my business, not yours!"

I beg to differ, hoarding *is* family business when loved ones must live under such grim conditions. Take Judith Scruggs' twelve year old son; he endured a home so messy, it's believed that he committed suicide because of it.[2]

While suicide is an extreme response, the child of a hoarder's is heavily impacted when his or her living space is commandeered by piles of junk that remove all semblance of a normal childhood. Imagine the inability to lie flat in one's bed because Dear Mummy has piled so much stuff atop it, and then refuses to permit any of it to be moved off! Imagine how it feels to play second-fiddle to a parent's trash in terms of passion and priority. Imagine how confusingly odd that the parent, who doesn't see their lifestyle as problematic, expects the child to go along as if nothing's amiss, and that this poor young soul is powerless to change things.

Plain and simple, it's abuse!

The occasional brave youngster risks bringing friends home, warns them what to expect, but is mortified by the reactions that ensue, including bullying, ostracism, and being the brunt of malicious gossip. Try it once, and most are hard-pressed to do so again. Then there's the cluttering parent who forbids their child to invite people over. Never allowed to bring home playmates, the kid may ultimately circumvent all discomfort by avoiding relationships altogether.

As if enduring the physical environment weren't bad enough, living in a home that's burgeoned out of control often means children are caught in the crossfire of escalating parental tensions. So how do children handle it?

At peril of alerting the authorities, some *do* complain. But when child welfare gets involved, the youngsters may be removed from the household.

All too often, after years of anger and shame, some children turn resentful and distance themselves. This distance may include severing relations. Worse yet, some become trapped, caring for their disabled, hoarding parent and grow into adulthood, still harnessed with the burden.

What is it like to have loving parents that one is ashamed of, and then to be mortified that one is ashamed?

Such stress and grief seems unimaginable!

As we know, when faced with a parent or two who hoard, many simply walk away. Yet others turn defensive and protect the problematic individual.

Should a family member stick around, there's a tendency to adopt a codependent dynamic. The codependent, in this case the non-hoarding spouse or child, may be reliant upon the hoarder for their identity and/or for approval, so they enable or acquiesce to the hoarder's habits and poor decisions. To survive their circumstances, this codependent individual becomes a people-pleaser, or a perfectionist, or a rescuer, and may also be prone to low self-esteem.

Furthermore, the codependent may protect their resident hoarder by conspiring with them to hide the problem. Overtly, they make excuses and minimize the impact of the hoarder's behavior on their lifestyle, while covertly expending enormous energies attempting to cope with their loved one's illness.

Melody Beattie, author of *Codependent No More,* popularized the term *codependency* in 1986. While not a hoarder and not raised by one, Melody *did* survive abandonment, kidnap, sexual abuse, drug and alcohol addiction, divorce, and worst of all, the death of her child. As a result of her insightful book, folks flock to Co-dependents Anonymous meetings for support. Modeled after Alcoholics Anonymous (AA), it's a fellowship that enjoins adherents to develop healthy relationships, and uses AA's twelve steps to manage codependent behaviors.

Then there's the self-help book, *Children of Hoarders: How to Minimize Conflict, Reduce the Clutter, and Improve Your Relationship*, which offers practical strategies to help the hoarder's offspring find sanity from the suffering they endured while growing up in a chaotic household.

Accommodating the hoarding parent may have become second nature for the child or spouse, yet this book encourages family to stop trying to get the parent to change, and also enjoins family to disengage from supporting the spouse or the parent's ongoing behaviors. Employ a Zen-like attitude—accept what is and what has been—the narrative encourages. Practice mindfulness by focusing awareness on the present moment, while acknowledging and accepting one's feelings, thoughts, and bodily sensations. Such actions can help alter one's relationship with the hoarder and heal past damage.[3]

⌂⌂ ⌂

With tangled branches to the hoarder's family tree commonplace, the hoarder's offspring live in fear, lest they inherit the trait. And many children, along with the hoarder's spouses devote their lives to protecting their family's secret. As family tries to shield the hoarder from condemnation and judgment, the child or spouse may decide to create revisionist stories, fabricating a nonexistent tidy life, while enduring the messiest, real-time existence imaginable.

To maintain the facade of normalcy, Kimberly Rae Miller established a decoy house, one with a normal looking exterior that she falsely claimed as home. As the daughter of a hoarder and of a compulsive shopper, on realizing that she lacked proper models with regard to overall hygienic behaviors, she secretly viewed YouTube videos and scrutinized product labels to learn how to clean and organize.

Revealing repeated incidents of shoveling out her parent's various homes, Kimberly Rae describes her search for answers in her memoir *Coming Clean*, Time and again, her beloved parents promise they'll stop collecting, yet nothing ever comes of it. There's good news, though; writing *Coming Clean* enabled her to come to terms with her difficult youth, so she now enjoys a modicum of peace.[4]

While Kimberly Rae is able to address the challenges of having two dysfunctional parents, many refuse to acknowledge the impact and magnitude of such dysfunction upon their lives. Another aspect of denial also occurs when family members dismiss scientific evidence acknowledging that hoarding has a physiological, as well as psychiatric basis. As a result there's a tendency to ascribe the hoarder's behavior to stubbornly volitional obnoxiousness.

⌂⌂ ⌂

If hoarding were elevated to the status of cancer or cardiac disease, it'd be more socially acceptable. Grasp that the disorder has a physiological basis, thereby making it a bonafide illness, and that attendant behaviors aren't performed to annoy or to alienate, and it's easier to muster compassion.

Compassion comes with realization that the hoarder's actions aren't rational, and that they aren't performed to incite, aggravate, or to harm others. Compassion arises as one tries to fathom the irresistible pull to collect. Compassion clicks into action with recognition that these folks are at the mercy of involuntary behaviors that cause relentless pain and isolation.

For the outsider, compassion means daring a glimpse at the immense toll the illness takes on the hoarder, on their family, as well as the community at large. Compassion's a tall order, though, when others are forced to wallow in filth that's imposed upon them!

While kin cannot control their out-of-control relative who hoards, they *can* and should seek help for themselves. Such help might include self-education, participation in support groups for the families of hoarders, seeking counseling for oneself, or attending the hoarder's therapy.

Educating oneself as to the complexities and nature of hoarding can make it easier to keep in contact. Sources that help with this include seeking out hoarding-related self-help books, and a plethora of online information. The

Web is rife with advice and direction in this regard, and the *San Francisco Bay Area Internet Guide for Extreme Hoarding Behavior* as well at the *International OCD Foundation* are two such sources for this.

Despite the existence of a smorgasbord of information and support, there's the occasional family member who sabotages the hoarder's treatment. Unconsciously, this individual may fear that the hoarder will change, and as a result, they can no longer be blamed for all family problems. In such instances, the hoarder—the *identified patient*, also called the *symptom bearer*, or the *presenting problem*—tends to act out the family's inner conflicts. As a result, self-scrutiny, as well as self care divert onto this problematic person, enabling family to avoid their own shortcomings.

Should the hoarder cease to collect, and all family dynamics shift. With the hoarder no longer to blame for every last problem, and all players must face their own long-festering dysfunctions.

In her role as crisis nurse, Janice has come across the occasional spouse willing to risk all to protect the hoarder. Audrey, for example, spent years helping her husband hoard, but then became too ill to keep pace with the ongoing influx. One day a neighbor called mental health, fretting that Audrey and her husband Charlie—who live, walled off from each other in separate parts of their house—hadn't been seen in weeks. The following is an account of Janice's subsequent visit.

"Anybody home?" Janice knocks.

No answer, she goes round the back, calls out, and knocks again. "Hello? Still, no answer; she tries the door, but it refuses to budge.

Off Janice goes to check with the referring neighbor who shares further details, "A while back, Audrey instructed Meals On Wheels to leave food at separate windows for her and Charlie. For a time, the trays disappeared, but they now go untouched. Charlie is demented, and Audrey's health is failing, so I worry about both of them."

Returned to the house, stacked newspapers, as if sentient beings, line the porch, and foil-covered trays, abuzz with flies, aggregate at the door.

Again, Janice calls out, "Hello, is anybody there?" She rattles and raps on windowpanes.

Ear pressed to the door, she hears a faint voice rasp, "I can't get to you."

"How about your husband," Janice calls back, "can he open up?"

"He's blocked in and can't get through," comes the reply.

"Sit tight," Janice hollers, "I'm going for help."

Within minutes police arrive, jimmy open a window, and climb inside.

Rustling, followed by thumps and crashes, and the door scrapes open. "She's in back," the officer announces, tossing objects aside to make a path.

Crab-walking sideways, Janice follows.

The officer pokes his head around a distant corner, then disappears.

Muted conversation, urgent and comforting on the officer's part, ensues. Then, amid much ado of shuffling and rustling, he returns. "Lady's barely alive. Paramedics are on their way. Follow me...she's down here."

Off they scrabble down the barely passable hall. Walls and floors obscured, jam-packed with junk, there are no crevices, nor smidgen of space, whatsoever, to add another twig as Janice and the officer clamber over slip-sliding piles of magazines and newspapers.

At hall's end sits Audrey, wedged between washer and dryer in the narrowest of spaces. The officer, shoving stuff out of the way, crouches alongside her. Janice, too, pushes junk aside and squats down.

Audrey can barely lift her head. "My chest hurts," she manages to rasp, "and I've got an ugly, lump beneath my rib cage. It's been there several months, and won't go away." Given the look of her swollen, fiery red legs, they seemed infected.

"Can you stand so we can get you out of here?" the officer queries.

"Never mind me..." she implores, "look to Charlie. He's stuck in the living room or thereabouts, and can't find his way out. Poor dear, he's demented, you know." Away the officer goes to check.

"How long since you've eaten?" asks Janice.

"I don't dare eat, 'cause food gives me such upset, and I can't get to the toilet."

Historically, Charlie's been the identified hoarder of the duo, but after fifty-two years of married life, at some point Audrey joined in to collect with a vigor equal to his. Now, with failing health, she declines medical attention for fear of being hospitalized, which means leaving Charlie unattended, and she refuses to entrust him to anyone else's care.

"Sir...Charlie, can you open the door?" the officer calls.

Excited guttural sounds burble up from the wall's other side.

Unable to get to him, the policeman smashes a window, tears the screen back, shoves the sash up, then slithers inside. "Ugh," he blurts, "there's stuff everywhere! I'm trying to clear space to the door."

Sounds—objects falling—he locates the husband. "How you doing? Stay there, Buddy, I'm coming to you." More rustling, several thuds, and a side door scrapes open.

Having crept back outside, Janice spies the emaciated, wild-eyed Charlie, who tries to speak, but merely flails.

Minutes later, paramedics arrive. Since they cannot move the gurney inside, they chuck debris out the door to create a path. Within minutes they reach Audrey to swiftly assess her; oxygen mask applied, then cart her out and onto the gurney.

As she's trundled into the ambulance, with the doors about to shut, Audrey musters a refusal. "Don't take me until you get Charlie. We've been together this long, so I insist we ride together."

Blinking and startled, as Charlie is led from the house and assisted into the vehicle, he lays eyes on his wife, claps hands and gurgles with delight.

Audrey hugs him, and cries, "He's all I have."

Doors shut, the ambulance departs.

Locating a scrap of wood, the police officer uses it to cover the broken window, securing a home this couple will never return to.

If you can't change 'em, you can join 'em, was possibly the most prudent strategy for Audrey. While this axiom may have saved their marriage, joining her hubby's penchant for collecting did nothing to prolong her life or improve their lifestyle.

Many a hoarder depends on the limit-setting capabilities of their non-hoarding partner to suppress their own urges. Whether the functional partner applies pressure, forcing the hoarder to organize and toss stuff, or keeps the home clean and organized on their own, the strain of such an existence causes the best or marriages to flounder.

Commonly, marriages between a hoarder and non-hoarder end in divorce. A big predictor as to whether the relationship survives depends largely on the severity of the clutter. If the hoarder devotes every waking minute to their obsession, they have little to offer in terms of intimacy and partnership, whereas the hoarder who collects part time, may have left over reserves to contribute to the relationship.

When the hoarder is in a partnership, they have the opportunity to *borrow* their mate's self-control and insight as a means of keeping their collecting under wraps. In the event of divorce, the death of a spouse, or when a child moves out, the hoarder's collecting is often free to go unchecked.

Steve, for instance, reveals that his mom's collecting escalated during his first semester away at college. Home at holiday break, he could no longer to carve sufficient sleeping space in his bedroom to lie down, and the shower stall was so crammed he had to wash up at a friend's.

As compulsions consume the hoarder and distract from their partner's needs, they have little extra to devote to family. As a result, the non-hoarder has four options: hoard alongside their spouse, or ignore the mess and live in the clutter, or constantly clean it up, or just depart.

Co-dependent to the nth degree, James tolerates his wife, Selma's, hoarding to an absurd extent. Almost cheerfully, he lives in a trash-filled home, most of it rendered unusable thanks to Selma's penchant. Whenever she gets an itch, he drives her to a favorite dumpster, helps her scavenge, crams found items into their car, and then drives home to unload their booty.

Some view James as extremely loyal, while others deem him disabled. *Folie à deux*—madness or emotional contagion shared by two—is a psychiatric syndrome in which delusional belief is transmitted from one individual to another. James, however, is quite self-aware and while he doesn't fit the precise diagnosis of sharing his wife's delusion, his means of coping is rather extreme.

Truly, he's adjusted well to his maladjusted existence!

"When I refused to permit my wife's behaviors," James explains, "she gave me the cold shoulder, which made it impossible to live with the hostility. So now that I've joined her, it's like we share a hobby. We get excited, all worked up as we strategize our next adventure, then go find stuff. After we bring it back, we discuss our finds, then plan the next trip. Because I've adapted, we get along just fine."

Indeed, James' enabling does make life tolerable. Ironically, however, his support circumvents any possible lifestyle changes that might improve his family's lot.

Another couple sets limits to positive effect. "Our marriage stays intact because I'm permitted one room to fill to my heart's delight," reports Adele, a young married hoarder. "I agree that the rest of our home has to stay tidy. Sean gets that I don't collect to be difficult, but because I have a problem. All he asks is that I respect our shared living space."

△△ △

In a duo-hoarder household, matters become exponentially more problematic. More challenging than that, one hoarding partner may seek help to curb their behaviors, yet the other hoarder does not.

The adult daughter of a hoarding couple recounts her parents' deterioration. "Years on end, Mom cared for our alcoholic, hoarder Dad, but their life worsened, big-time, when she joined him in drinking, and then compulsively made mail order purchases. At some point Mom became too demented to organize or to manage the ongoing influx. Then they began to isolate, never left the house and cut off contact; they even refused to talk by phone."

The children arranged for grocery delivery, along with Meals on Wheels. Often, the parents' phone got shut off for non-payment, and utility service providers habitually gave the children a courtesy call when electricity and heat were about to be terminated.

Because the kids nagged, the couple refused to let them visit. When they *did* try to check on their parents, the door went unanswered. Forced to peek in windows, the visuals appalled. Once fastidious to a fault, their mom now left the home a-jumble of take-out-food boxes, newspapers, cans, and cartons. Even from outside, the place reeked of rotting food.

It took their dad's death for them to fully grasp the extent of the problem. When the children gained access, they found entrances into rooms impossibly blocked and the entire place jammed with debris. Dutifully, they dutifully cleared and scrubbed everything. Yet months later, it had to be cleaned again.

Frequently, Mom groused that unwelcome strangers snuck in to make those messes, and accused her children of taking things. Often, she called 911 to complain of theft. Tired of wild goose chases, law enforcement threatened to file charges against her, as it's illegal to call 911 without just cause.

Tensions grew as Mom verbally abused her offspring and threatened to disown them. To the amazement of all, she even managed the wherewithal to initiate a restraining order intent on barring all contact. Ultimately, she proved too disorganized to follow through with it.

The children, determined to weather the abuse, steadfastly tried to help in all ways possible. "It's been rough enough just dealing with Mom," her daughter shares, "but it would have been awful if we'd fought among ourselves. It helps immensely that all of us are on the same page and support each other's efforts."

When families are at odds about how to relate to their resident family hoarder, the conflicting perspectives can tear them apart. Far too often, a family member will take charge of finances, only to squander the money. Worse yet, a frustrated adult child may turns abusive or neglectful. Both scenarios are against the law, and are punishable crimes.

Back to our story: the children hung in there, weathering three years of varied and assorted crises, until mom finally got psychiatrically hospitalized. During her stay, she busily aggregated fellow patients' belongings, cluttering her room with their junk. Thankfully, when placed on an antipsychotic medication, her paranoia and disorganization diminished to some extent.

Post-discharge, much to her children's delight, their mom kept taking the prescribed medication. With her abusiveness dulled, she eventually welcomed contact, enjoyed her children's visits, and grudgingly permitted them to clean and maintain her home. Despite improvement, however, she kept right on collecting.

CHAPTER 11

Scraping Out the Dead—Hoarders Who Die Amidst Their Stuff

"Each year around 50,000 people die in New York, some alone and unseen. Yet death, even in such forlorn form can cause a surprising amount of activity. Sometimes, along the way, life's secrets are revealed."

—N.R. Kleinfield

"The Lonely Death of George Bell," by N. R. Kleinfield, *The New York Times*, October 17, 2015[1], is excerpted and adapted as follows:

"They found him in the living room, crumpled up on the mottled carpet. The police did. Sniffing a fetid odor, a neighbor had called 911. The apartment, located in north-central Queens, was in an unassuming building on 79th Street in Jackson Heights.

"The apartment belonged to a George Bell. He lived alone. Thus the presumption was that the corpse also belonged to George Bell. It was a plausible supposition, but it remained just that, for the puffy body on the floor was decomposed and unrecognizable."

Following up on a neighbor's complaint, firefighters jimmied a door open, allowing police to squeeze inside a space so heavily laden with junk that clearly the occupant had been a hoarder. The human remains got zipped into a bag, and then went off to the medical examiner, who slid it into a refrigerated drawer to await confirmation as to its identity. In the subsequent search for identifying information, detectives on the scene managed to scoop up papers containing names and phone numbers, and later called them all, but got nothing.

Every county has its own public administrator who steps in to manage estates when no will or no known heirs exist. So it fell to this department to tidy up the loose ends pertaining to the corpse, presumed to be George Bell.

When unable to locate next of kin who might identify the body, formal confirmation is required. For this purpose, fingerprints were taken from the remains, which posed a bit of a challenge, because of their deteriorated condition. These prints were then sent to city, state, and federal databases for verification.

The medical examiner's office also took chest X-rays, but needed earlier ones for comparison. With no idea which doctors the man had seen, staff contacted all medical facilities within the vicinity of his apartment, asking if a George Bell had ever dropped in.

Meanwhile, investigators working for the Public Administrator donned hazmat suits, along with rubber gloves and booties, to further mine the apartment for clues. Their mission: to find a will, or to locate financial statements, or an address book, or a laptop, or maybe even a cellphone, or possibly find the deed to a cemetery plot, and/or get a gander at family photos.

In this process, they retrieved a small amount of cash, along with a designer watch, and miscellaneous papers. Hung from apartment walls were a bear's head, steer horns, along with pictures of military planes and warships. One photo sequence, showing a parachutist while landing, bore a certificate that recorded George Bell's first jump in 1963.

The apartment was a disarray of food cartons and pizza boxes; shelves were stacked with music tapes and videos. Half a dozen unopened boxes contained ironing board covers. Multiple other boxes contained unused Christmas lights, and four new tire pressure gauges dotted the scene. Best of all, they unearthed a will. Dated 1982, it split George Bell's estate equally between three men and one woman—all of unknown relation—and specified that his body be cremated.

Grim as the place was, the Public Administrator had seen worse, including an apartment so crammed with belongings that the tenant died standing upright, and remained thus, unable to collapse to the floor.

⌂⌂ ⌂

So, what sort of person might be willing to scavenge through the life of another for a living?

One who possesses a strong stomach, no doubt. A fearless soul, who will sift through someone's detritus, taking into stride the mundane and odd relics that reveal themselves. And perhaps this sort of person also doesn't want to die and be forgotten as so many are.

In addition to the growing numbers of decluttering businesses, there are disaster cleanup specialists who offer specific, unique cleaning services. Some provide crime scene cleanup in the event of murder or suicide and are mindful to restore the site in as respectful a manner as possible. To work in this capacity, staff must be trained in the removal of blood-borne pathogens, as well as grasp the proper handling of bodily fluids that can transmit disease. Others of these businesses deal with cleanup following a natural disaster, including debris removal and water extraction.

Picture for a moment the icky sensations and foul odors as one scoops through the mess. Rats scurry out from rotting cardboard; food puddles turn to mold on countertops; long neglected floorboards collapse as they're traversed; and there's a full, but unflushed leaky toilet that has overflowed.

Certainly, this work is not for the faint of heart! Instances where a hoarder's home is cleaned, not only do these workers remove debris and possessions, they scrape up animal carcasses as well as feces—animal and human—trap vermin, and remove mildew, rot, as well as mold. As these people work, care must be taken to avoid injury they may include needle sticks and debris that crashes down upon them. Occasionally, while sifting through hazardous trash, they even come upon the dead.

My Internet search reveals multiple tales of hoarders who die in their messes. One reclusive woman died in her basement after the first floor of her Connecticut home collapsed beneath the weight of her stuff. According to report, the place contained clutter piled to the ceiling, which posed such a hazard that rescuers were forced to abandon their initial attempt to find the 66-year-old.[2]

⌂⌂ ⌂

It's tough enough to earn one's livelihood getting paid to sift through another's hoard, but it has to be to be devastating to be that family member who goes through debris in search of a loved one who has died, and then must cope with the messy aftermath. Greg Martin did exactly that.

While trying to locate his 83-year-old mother, Martin walked atop junk piles, until he found her body. With the floor completely buried beneath stacks of magazines, papers, books and clothes, he then spent at least eight more months cleaning out her home.

Martin's progress slowed, because he, like many children of hoarders, felt the pull of certain items found in his mother's hoard. While he managed to throw out, recycle, and donate many years worth of clothing, costume jewelry, and trash, he also kept a lot—including an envelope of clothing tags from garments his mom bought for him. He also held on to hundreds of vinyl records and, for some reason, an outdated tape recorder with leaky, corroded batteries. According to his view, the entire experience afforded an opportunity for him to acknowledge—and to reject—his own hoarding tendencies.³

"I don't think [hoarders] want to leave their children with a mess," says Dr. Fugen Neziroglu, a psychologist with New York's Bio Behavioral Institute. "They don't go through in their minds what's going to happen with the clutter, or what the kids are going to do with it."

To circumvent becoming saddled with a whole lot of trash, Neziroglu recommends that the topic be broached with the hoarder as part of a supportive family intervention. Encouragement and love, she recommends, are essential, rather than deploying anger and blame. This gathering is most promising if a subsequent follow-up visit is made to see a therapist.⁴

Easier said than done!

With no magic answers or wonder drug in hand, relatives often retreat in frustrated fury to wait it out, and end up dealing with the hoard "when the time comes." For those bequeathed these horrific messes, processing grief can become quite the challenge.

Returned to the topic of dead bodies; how long can a corpse go undetected?

Gladys Bergmeier held on to her dead mother's remains at least twenty years. Subsequent to her husband's death in the late 1980s, Bergmeier turned reclusive and proceeded to pack her home to the brim with newspapers, plastic bags, and other assorted trash.

At some point, the mother, also named Gladys, moved in with her. But when Gladys Senior went missing, relatives wondered what became of her. Because the daughter avoided contact, they eventually stopped asking.

Gladys the elder, it seems, hadn't gone anywhere. After the daughter's death at age 75, Mom's decayed body was found sandwiched between a wall and a bed; wrapped in fabric, as well as trash bags, the corpse had mummified.[5]

Then there's Bill James, who reported his wife, Billie Jean, missing. Authorities looked for her with search dogs, and even flew helicopters overhead, using infrared technology, to no avail. Months passed and still Bill had no idea where his wife had gone. One day, however, he spotted her feet jutted out from beneath a ceiling high junk pile.[6]

Hard to imagine how he endured the smell of her rotting corpse!

△△ △

With regard to George Bell, the Public Administrator finally located the individuals named in his will and proceeded to send out letters, requesting that they get in touch. The only one who replied, noted that he hadn't spoken with George in some time. Despite their remote relationship, George named this fellow as executor, but the man deferred the task to the public administrator.

Although George was known to have a will, the County was still tasked to find family, lest the will be contested. Turns out he had five living relatives: none had been in contact for decades.

At some point, the medical examiner filed an unverified certificate of death, noting the cause of demise as hypertension and atherosclerotic cardiovascular disease, with obesity as a significant contributing factor. When a corpse's identity remains unconfirmed, cremation isn't permitted. Should there be a mix-up or if facts get scrambled, should a body turn to ash it cannot be reassembled to double check. So George's corpse, or what was assumed to be his, waited still longer.

Months along, a downstairs neighbor complained that liquids from George's apartment were leaking through the ceiling, and that creatures could be heard scuttling about. A clean out company then went in and found the refrigerator unplugged, with rotting food dripping from the inside, along with an infestation of cockroaches. As a result, they removed what remained of the mess and clutter.

In situations where a home's contents are devoid of worth, as George's was, clean out companies simply dispose of the belongings. With regard to George's apartment, workers kept some items, including a set of Marilyn Monroe commemorative plates, an unopened twelve pack of Nike socks, a few model cars, and sponges. One fellow grabbed a new pair of work boots, slid them on and cleaned the apartment while wearing them.

By my guess, George wasn't a hoarder of the highest magnitude, but more of a specialist hoarder or a collector who'd slipped into sloth due to a combination of physical decline and possible depression. At any rate, he didn't exactly sound like the worst of the worst.

⌂⌂ ⌂

Back to the search for George's old x-rays; in a process somewhat like trying to pinpoint the far end of eternity, the medical examiner kept calling around. Then finally, wonder of wonders, he lucked out.

A radiology office, it seems, possessed a set of George Bell's chest x-rays. After a bit of fumbling and confusion, the film deemed a match. As a result, four months after arrival, they could formally identify the corpse as that of George, so according to his stated request, he could now be cremated.

While some prefer to have their ashes scattered, others opt to have their cremains stored in a columbarium, which is a room or building that houses funeral urns that have been tucked into wall niches. With cremation complete, a shoebox-size urn got placed in such a space, with the identifier, *George M. Bell Jr., 1942-2014.*

Regarding the ongoing search for the rest of those named in George's will, the Public Administrator learned that two were deceased, and the remaining were surprised to learn of George Bell's bequest. A few weeks before George's death, one of them spoke with him by phone, while the other hadn't been in touch for years. At some point, word came that one of the remaining two was newly deceased; given that she'd outlived George, her estate would receive her share of the proceeds.

George's Toyota, with merely 3000 miles on it, sold at auction for $9,500, which meant the final accounting of the estate came to $540,000. Subtracting commissions and fees, a mere $264,000 remained to be split between the one living recipient and the heirs of the other.

With the loose ends of George's demise resolved, I began to wonder just who this man was: *Had he loved and been loved? Was he a good man, was he mostly ordinary, did he have any odd quirks, and what did he care about? Mostly, did it really matter in the big or small scale of things that he'd even existed?* And, *Why did he die so alone?*

Turns out, George was especially attached to his parents. His dad was a tool-and-die machinist, and his mother worked as a seamstress. After high school, George apprenticed with his father, but later established his own moving company. Much of his life, he slept on the living room sofa, while his parents claimed the bedroom. Even after their deaths, he continued to sleep there. His father died young and as his mom aged, she became crippled with arthritis, so George cared for her until the end.

While in his twenties he dated a woman, whom he planned to marry, but ended the engagement, never to have another serious relationship again. The two kept in touch, though, and George named her in his will.

Thickset, brawny, probably weighing about 210 pounds, he was known as *Big George,* and eventually he managed to push the scale to 350. He had diabetes, and shoulder pain, both required medications. When a spinal injury forced him to cease work, he lived off Social Security disability and received a pension.

For a time, he socialized, yet friends found him difficult to know. During the latter part of his life, he mostly isolated. Eight years ago, when his final remaining pal hadn't heard from him and went to check, George shooed the friend away.

So onward George traipsed, divorced from human contact. Mostly, he stayed cloistered inside; neighbors heard deliveries of takeout meals. Then one day he died alone, no one to assist or to hold his hand, nobody to even know that he'd gone.[7]

When a person dies without family or friends, there's no memorial, no service, and no kind words are said. However, I had to wonder if any hoarder in their dying moments ever thought with satisfaction, *At long last, I have everything I could possibly need!*

On the other hand, as the soul of a hoarder ascends, they might take a swipe to grasp that final mouthful of air and entertain one last terminally fading thought, *Best not be caught without!*

CHAPTER 12

Got Affluenza?—The Spiritual Ramifications of Our Junk

"In this world there are only two tragedies. One is not getting what one wants and the other is getting it."

—Oscar Wilde.

AF-FLU-EN-ZA DEFINED: 1. THE BLOATED, sluggish, and unfulfilled feeling that results from efforts to keep up with the Joneses. 2. An epidemic of stress, overwork, waste and indebtedness caused by the dogged pursuit of the American Dream. 3. An unsustainable addiction to economic growth.

My Husband's Under Here Somewhere

For purposes of this book, *affluenza* is seen as a painful, contagious, socially transmitted malady that involves the dogged pursuit of things that result in consumption overload, which then leads to debt, anxiety, and waste.[1]

One bears the affliction of affluenza if their symptoms include the purchase of more shoes than can possibly be worn in several lifetimes; or if one proudly pays premium price for a T-shirt bearing some corporate logo; or when down in the dumps, one shops till they drop; or if its routine to make only the minimum credit card payment; or if it's essential to purchase that expensive evening gown, in hopes that a fancy party will materialize; and finally, if self-worth is solely measured by what one owns.

Affluenza is further manifest by the willingness to slave an entire lifetime at a detestable job for the privilege of wallowing in gobs of stuff. The use and abuse of credit cards are also part of the disorder, for they create the illusion that one can afford all sorts of objects that humans, as a rule, are better off without.

Reverend Billy Talen, hybrid street preacher, televangelist, with a dollop of Elvis tossed in, is the subject of the documentary, *What Would Jesus Buy?* Reverend Billy, along with his *Not Buying-It* band, and the churchly *Stop Shopping Choir*, preach of the impending *Shopocalypse*, which heralds humanity's demise from consumerism, over-consumption, and the fires of eternal debt.

Film footage shows Reverend Billy as he delves into the role that sweatshops and Big-Box stores play in America's habitual, massive consumerism. With this narrative as his soapbox, the Reverend gets himself arrested and rearrested, time and again. Anti-consumer advocate that Reverend Billy is, the film's director Rob Van Alkemade notes that his subject's message is somewhat hypocritical, as "...Wal-Mart pushes half of their DVD sales."[2]

During hunter-gatherer times, humans worked approximately ten hours a week. Back then, folks possessed far less stuff, lived cooperatively and collectively, and were deeply connected to each other, as well as to the land and to the seasons. After a time, people aggregated in small villages where residents remained intricately intertwined, and lives were defined by the nature of one's labor, or by the works of one's forefathers.

Family roots ran deep in those times. A man was known as *John the butcher, son of Abraham*. Most simply wished to survive and to leave offspring, who would also survive, hopefully in relative comfort and ease.

As basic survival needs were met, life grew more complex. New goals arose, creating increasing, never before heard of demands and expectations, and then life's pace sped up.

Nowadays, we're hard-pressed to know our neighbor's name to call out a hello, and certainly don't feel friendly enough to invite them over. Given the rat race that's overtaken us, most of the time we're simply too tired to bother.

Mom prepares quick-fix meals that the family chows down; nobody at the table makes eye contact or engages in camaraderie. Come Sunday morning, Dad sequesters in the john with newsprint or tablet in hand to snatch a moment's peace. Yet the news he reads, with all its impossibly horrific dilemmas, overwhelms. Coffee is slurped up, then everyone rushes off, going hither and thither at a killingly frantic pace. Later, the adults imbibe alcohol or takes drugs to deaden the senses, then clamber into bed to snooze fitfully. Come morning, they awaken to a jangly alarm, lever upright, and run off to join the rat race yet again.

Public school education manages to shape us into obedient consumers. Giving us something to look forward to in the form of material objects, makes us easier to control and the promise of having makes it easier to tolerate our soul-sucking jobs. Like rats on a wheel, running frantically in an endless loop, we work to amass as much money as possible, to then waste it on rubbish.

To consume is ingrained in our culture. Duct tape notwithstanding, after 9/11 hit, President George Walker Bush instructed our citizenry to shop as a patriotic act.

Incur significant credit card debt or unable to pay the mortgage?

Not a problem...just declare bankruptcy, as Donald Trump has done, then wait a few years, and begin the cycle over again. "I used the law [declared bankruptcy] four times [actually six] and made a tremendous thing," says Trump. "I'm in business. I did a very good job."

That's the *American Way!*

Given that its the overarching American attitude to spend, quite possibly you, too, embrace consumerism and view such acts as patriotic. Decline to enslave oneself by going into debt—but opt to save instead—and one is accused of harming the economy.

There's also the prevalent message to spend a gob of money during the Holidays in order to demonstrate sufficient love of family. Better yet, max out those credit cards in order to be seen as *really* sacrificing for those beloveds!

⌂⌂ ⌂

In the early 1900s, American technology created a vast array of shiny new baubles for our amusement and consumption. Advertising then got into the act and set about to convince us that we had serious need for these things. As a result, modern day capitalism emerged.

"Advertising," Calvin Coolidge once declared, "is the method by which desire is created for better things."

Indeed, advertising offers a false promise of happiness and manages to polish absolutely everything, including the dust motes. Messages imparted by men such as Don Draper in the TV series *Mad Men,* spawn and spread relentless images in an effort to shape us into compulsive consumers.

Advertising skillfully raises our anxiety by speaking to our low self-esteem. Brainwashed to be perpetually insecure and dissatisfied, we're encouraged to strive for inclusion. As a result, we're chronically restless and dissatisfied, and have become a society of folks who have-a-little-but-always-want-more.

These days, a triumvirate that includes capitalism, mass media, and advertising conspires to manipulate public opinion. To that end, they effectively create new demands and new dissatisfactions that can only ostensibly be assuaged by consuming more commodities.

From birth, we're pushed to purchase on impulse, and to take a swift detour around all semblance of thoughtful calculation. Having been oh-so-carefully fine-tuned, we're further instilled with the inability to tolerate delayed gratification. Early programming, coupled with this pervasive gotta-have-it-now mentality, also engenders our sense of entitlement.

A handsome couple of my acquaintance, kind, generous, loving to a fault, lives in an upscale neighborhood in an enormous, elegantly appointed home. When their snazzy Mercedes conked out on the freeway, the wife hopped the guardrail, marched across to the nearby auto lot and bought a spanking new Prius, thereby placing sizable debt on her credit card, without giving the matter a second thought.

At first blush this duo has it all, but their dozen-or-so credit cards are maxed out, and their home is on its fourth refinance. They're so deep in debt, they've borrowed from their children's college funds and have no idea if they'll ever crawl out from the pit they've dug. But do they cut up those credit cards, tend their yard without a gardener, or let the maid go?

Nope, no way!

Wealth, status, and power are accepted cultural symbols of success. Even the less affluent surround themselves with luxuries previously unknown to past civilizations.

The things we possess announce to one and all how very chic we are. Display of our stuff wins admiration, or at very least, helps us appear acceptable. Imbued with an urgent need to keep up, we search for the perfect home in that hoity-toity neighborhood, accept a mortgage we cannot handle, covet the latest technology, or the neighbor's new Maserati...all at huge cost to our personal values.

So how does *affluenza* apply to hoarding?

Many so-called *normals* smugly see packrats as being in the throes some hideous disease. Face it, though, most all of us are acquisitive to varying degrees.

The distinction between obsession and normalcy blurs when one can no longer park the car in the garage because it's too jammed with stuff, or when one must duck and cover every time a closet door is opened, or if one habitually brings home yard sale junk that will never be used. If you're in the ranks of the aforementioned, the distinction between some oddball hoarder and self is razor-thin.

According to activist Noam Chomsky the media uses our acquisitiveness to divide us. "The culture of narcissism," he notes, "and the *me generation* that swept the country in the 1970s were purely fictitious. I'm convinced that the whole thing was crafted by the public-relations industry to tell mainly young people, 'Look, this is who you are—you don't care about all this solidarity and sympathy and helping people.'

"'You guys can't do anything, you're alone, you're each separate; you've never achieved anything, and you never *will* achieve anything.' Of course they tell us that, 'You don't want to achieve anything, all you want to do is consume more.'"[3]

What does it say about us that, television watching aside, shopping is our favorite national pastime?

It says that hoarders aren't alone in their grasping rapaciousness. Dare to hold up a mirror, and one's own rampant materialism is reflected back.

During my work with hoarders, I pondered whether hoarding was possibly emblematic with regard to the cultural creep of emptiness. Distill it down, and hoarders, who never feel full emotionally, intellectually, or physically complete serve as the proverbial canaries in the coal mine, as they manifest excess that so many of us also gorge upon. Be ye hoarder or not, clearly, many feel the lack.

"I am convinced," writes Rabbi Harold Kushner, "that it is not the fear of death, of our lives ending, that haunts our sleep, so much as the fear that our lives will not have mattered; that as far as the world is concerned we might as well never have lived. What we miss in our lives, no matter how much we have, is that sense of meaning."4

Deep in our heart of hearts, meaning is what humans truly long for.

So, if meaning and value cannot be retrieved from the things we possess, why do we live thus?

To *have* in our culture, means success. Not having signifies failure. *Having* for many matters more than our relationships, and more than our health. Indeed, most of us seek to avoid familiarity with our inner selves by rushing about, keeping as busy as possible. Shopping offers a dandy means by which to do so.

As we obsess about *having*, however, we exclude our spiritual aspect.

Remember Maxine from Chapter Five?

Daily, she loads up her Jaguar with thrift store finds, drives home, dumps her booty in the yard, and then returns to do the same all over again. Never mind that her home and yard are filled-to-overflowing, or that her neighbors are riled, and that her home is unlivable; there's never a moment when she's satisfied.

When making a purchase, she *does* claim to enjoy a brief high. Yet, she also admits to vast, overarching emptiness. "Hoarding," she notes, "merely deadens the pain of living."

Sheer anticipation of buying may be a source of pleasure, yet the moment one takes possession, feelings about that object, one so deeply desired, tend to shift. Shortly after it's possessed, a sense of loss or a twinge of emptiness arises, and the value imbued within it diminishes.

As a result, that gotta-have-it doohickey gets set on the shelf, alongside all the other gizmos that were once so coveted, which then frees one up to shine that attentive beacon onto yet another object again. Keep following this incessant drive, and the inner self is lost.

It's easy to attribute this urge to thoroughly fill up time and space with possessions to a lousy childhood, or to a job that lacks meaning, or to a general malaise of spirit. When dissatisfied, many pursue having more, yet something's terribly amiss if that gnawing hunger is never sated. Only the rare soul dares examine why this is so.

Yet, we can certainly try to do so by posing questions: *How much of your own life is devoted to the relentless pursuit of having more?* And, further, *Are all those things you possess actually enjoyable?*

Affluenza, a disease caused by materialism, is a malaise that affects many. Those badly bitten tend to define who they are in terms of what they have. Possession offers up a false sense of self-worth, and similar to Maxine, helps insulate from the pain of living.

Using objects as surrogate companions, Maxine, who longs for love, settles for a house full of junk instead. Unwilling to reach out to her children and risk rejection, she readily admits that shopping poses far less of a threat.

Sure, some of the things we possess give promise of security, or status, or offer aesthetic pleasure. Certainly, many of them make life easier. And a sense of power can derive from the things we own. So if objects hold power, it stands to reason, that the more one possesses, the more powerful one becomes.

Joanie, a 56-year-old hoarder, shared the following: "There isn't a moment that I don't run this loop of inner dialogue—it happens even as I sleep—and goes like this: Another day and here's the same mess. Why can't I get organized like others can? I'm not lazy, stingy or stupid, so how did I get like this?

"In all these boxes are my fulfilled and unfilled dreams, my memories of people that I loved and lost, my attempts to live a decent life, and all my good intentions. It wounds my childish ego to admit that all this flimsy evidence is the sum total of what I have to show for my existence, and really, it matters to no one but me."

Clutter and excess aren't limited to the material realm. Excess includes that very crammed social calendar; one dotted with pointless social events. Excess involves television watching for hours on end; or making lunch dates with unlikable, gossipy friends. Excess also includes spending every leisure moment traipsing the shopping mall. Furthermore, excess means engaging in activities that drain, rather than fulfill.

A cluttered life may include perpetual attendance at self-help workshops. Clutter can encompass days filled with endless projects. Clutter means embracing an obsessive hobby that distracts from one's true purpose. Clutter even includes food binges, followed by gagging and vomiting. Clutter is about fear of the future and fear of not having. Clutter wreaks havoc; it's everything that distracts, nags and lurks in the recesses of junked-up minds. In the end, clutter drags one down, till the soul is deadened.

For the serious collector, competition may rear up to the extent that others are viewed as rivals. See…even the things we own compete for our time and attention. With buckets full of time spent saving up for, and then having, the more objects one owns, the more energy one must expend. After all, our things must be maintained, managed, and protected. So forget making meaningful contact. Most of us are too busy amassing and striving to connect anyhow.

Of greater concern, with consumerism rampant within Western culture, out extravagant abuse of natural resources depletes and degrades this beloved earth of ours. Plastics and other objects that never decompose clog the landfill, and chemicals pollute our groundwater, as we busily deforest the Amazon, and scrape away the ozone layer. Meanwhile, less developed countries strive to catch up so they, too, can destroy and pillage.[5]

Buddha warned: *Resist what is and suffer. Better to accept what is and live happily.* The takeaway from this: live life to the fullest and accept what comes, while making as small a footprint as possible.

Except that's no easy task.

Refuse to amass, and one must face the angst that's easily avoided while rushing about to aggregate. Quite possibly, the pain that arises is that of self-alienation.

Dare to examine the relationship had with one's stuff and ask: *Do I benefit from having this item? Does it serve or enslave me? And is it really, truly necessary?*

As answers arise, probe further: *Why do I think I need to keep it? And will I miss it if it's gone?*

Delve still deeper to inquire: *What do I avoid by slobbering over this particular gizmo? Does it distract from my life's real purpose? Does this object weigh me down,? Or do I hold onto it in an attempt to fill a void or to impress?* Furthermore: *What matters most: to amass a whole lot of or to host a rich inner life?*

△△ △

Ordinary pursuits, collecting as a means of saving nostalgia—be they comic books, Beanie Babies, baseball cards—are often attempts to reproduce momentary warmth or relatedness. Yet pleasure and happiness aren't external, out of control forces. They arise from within.

By seeking happiness or security through the possession of material goods, many grow distant from their innate selves. With hoarding at the extreme, all obsession to possess derails and distracts us from what matters most; a life of meaning and connection.

No matter how much one has, the stuff amassed merely keeps us occupied, preoccupied, and befuddled. Same as the hoarder who cannot enjoy what he or she has, a life spent in the pursuit of having more causes us to lose track of why we exist.

So, then…when is enough, enough?

Personally, I don't shop unless a specific need arises and I also make a point of living within my means. Everything I own fits into my 25 year old Volvo. I recycle, buy second-hand items, and appreciate all I have, using things until they turn to tatters.

My lifestyle choice is not ordinary. To change how one lives requires going against the grain. To decide that one has enough stuff is a fearless, fully honest act; one which requires conscious, deliberate lifestyle modification.

Do any of us know someone who has divested of their stuff and is utterly content?

The happiest folks aren't the wealthiest or the most famous, and certainly aren't those who possess the most. Happy people are free and unfettered; they attend to each moment as it arises and are content with what is.

Regardless as to life circumstances, even in the face of dire, tragic events, it's possible to choose one's mindset.

How about the young Catholic Ettie Hillesum, who voluntarily joined the Jews in Auschwitz during World War II?

Entering the very place most would deem hell, she didn't suffer, at least not that she'd admit. Relying on her faith, and by exerting conscious control, she chose joy and contentment, and even claimed to be bliss-filled.

Hard to imagine finding deep, abiding love and inner peace while enduring such a nightmare!

"I live in constant intimacy with God...," she credited.

Mind you, this bright shiny soul died in the Camp.

Minimalism, originally a technique or style of music, literature, or design, is characterized by sparse simplicity. Those who live a minimalist lifestyle pare down, freeing themselves from the trappings of our consumer culture.

Adhering to this style of living doesn't make it inherently wrong to own material possessions, yet the minimalist believes that inevitable problems and complications arise when one possesses things. Assign too much meaning to our stuff, they opine, and we forsake our health, our relationships, our passions, along with our personal growth, as well as the time and ability to contribute beyond ourselves.

So, what's the point of such deprivation?

The following duo offers about the best answer I've come upon: At age 30, Joshua Fields Millburn and Ryan Nicodemus walked away from successful corporate careers, scrapping most of their possessions in order to focus on what's truly important. Although they seemingly had it all, both worked long hours, wasted money, lived paycheck to paycheck, and incurred debt. One lost a marriage and both men fell into discontent and depression.

In their book, *Minimalism: Live a Meaningful Life* the authors explore their troubled pasts and share how they found contentment. By eliminating all excess, they now focus on their mental, physical and spiritual health. When rid of life's trappings, their relationships, passions, and life-affirming endeavors have had ample room and time to blossom.[6]

Minimalists such as these whittle down until they have only the barest essentials—imagine possessing merely fifteen objects! They live in tiny houses, do not collect as a hobby or otherwise, have two changes of clothes, are car-free, and make a limited impact on the environment. In the process of shedding, joy, along with a sense of purpose, fulfillment, and freedom now abound.

Happiness, for these people, no longer rests with the material realm, but involves living to the fullest. Divested of most all trappings, they are able to focus on what's important and pursue purpose-driven lives. While adhering to this lifestyle isn't everyone's cup of tea, embracing simplicity can restore sanity and balance.

As he packs to travel, success guru, James Altucher, can fit all his worldly possessions into a small carry-on bag. Some time back, when the lease expired on his apartment, he dumped or donated virtually everything he owned, then stayed with friends or used Airbnb rentals for a time. Not that he's down on his luck, this former venture capitalist and financial wizard simply practices what he preaches.

"I have ambition," he says, "to have no ambition."[7]

Years ago, he and his wife lived in a 5,000-square-foot Tribeca loft that he bought for $1.8 million and then spent another $1 million to renovate. At that time, he enjoyed frequent weekend jaunts to Atlantic City via helicopter to play several hands of poker. Despite his lavish lifestyle, all his luxuries failed to fill the emotional void.

"I felt like I needed $100 million to be happy," Altucher admits. "So I just started investing in all these other companies, and they were just stupid companies. Zero of these investments worked out."[8]

As his fortunes collapsed, he was forced to sell his apartment at a substantial loss, but then set about again to reclaim his wealth. With his sights set on the stock market, alas his fortunes crumbled once again. "I've made every mistake in the book...." he admits.[9]

At some point, he found a sizable audience of those whose dreams and wealth had also disappeared, and they, too, were looking to figure out their lives. Writing candidly about his own triumphs and failures in his book, *Choose Yourself,* Altucher lets people know that it's possible to succeed on their own terms. His philosophy is the following: "If you don't choose the life you want to live, chances are, someone else is going to choose it for you. And the results are probably not going to be pretty."[10]

A key tenet is his wellness regimen. Its *four pillars of happiness* include the following admonishments: eat well, go to bed early and get up at the crack of dawn, break a sweat at least once a day; surround yourself with people you love, and those who love you; come up with list of ten creative ideas each day to exercise the brain; and take time to note what you're grateful for.

Unlike most gurus, Altucher's life is a work in progress and he openly shares his ups and downs in his blog, *The Altucher Report*. Allowing his followers to witness his own journey in real time as he adjusts, modifies, and forges ahead, he discusses what works for him and what does not.[11]

Divested of her name and all worldly possessions, a silver-maned woman, self-dubbed the *Peace Pilgrim*, trekked 25,000 miles across the United States on foot. As an ambassador of world peace, her simple and profound message touched the hearts and minds of thousands.

Most of us could take a page from this woman's journey. One small way to do so includes the following: When an object is acquired, take a moment to pause and relish it.

Getting rid of clutter doesn't mean that deprivation need be the end result. Indeed, lightening up means setting oneself free.

"As I surround myself solely with things I love," comments Annette, consummate Goodwill scavenger, "my need for stuff has ebbed. Better yet, as I simplify and divest, I have more space to love myself and more time for others."

Opposite of the hoarder is the Zen Buddhist who generally lives a bare-bones existence. Buddhists, some pathologically frugal, embrace simplicity and emptiness, and strive to be satisfied with life as it manifests.

Although not a Buddhist, Janice's multi-windowed house is flooded with natural light, and many joy-filled paintings grace its walls. Emanating a pervasive lush feel, it's a place where intense color and bird song abound. Each time my sister returns to it, no matter how brief the trip, she attests to an uplift. "Our house is amazingly peaceful, as well as comforting, and healing.," she says. "So much so, that John [her husband] and I joke about tossing a coin as to whose turn it is to leave to run errands."

Theoretically, home is a sacred space; at least it should be. As a reflection of one's inner being—the status of one's soul—it's where the presence or lack of spiritual essence is made manifest.

It's my belief that we attract the surroundings and life circumstances that we think we deserve. Since a cluttered living space bespeaks of the messiness within, quite possibly, we don't feel worthy of living otherwise. As a result of this disempowered outlook, havoc, confusion, and misery rule our lives.

The decision to tidy up a filthy, clutter-filled home can transform confusion into clarity, and shame into self-esteem. Should a space be cleared, if one's overall mindset stays firmly entrenched, clutter—as the external manifestation of one's beliefs—crops back up, yet again.

Yet during my years on this planet, I've come to understand that confusion and misery can be a choice for most. Should an overcrowded schedule or irrelevant trivia clog one's existence, it can be quite the revelation to note that its possible to choose otherwise. Going a step further, by surrounding myself with needy, difficult people, I avoid tending to my own needs.

As the inspiration for Orson Welles' 1941 film, *Citizen Kane*, Charles Foster Kane-ostensibly, the William Randolph Hearst character—is sent away as a child to be raised by his mother's banker. When Kane, who never reconciles this loss, comes into a seemingly endless fortune, he grows callous and arrogant. Compulsively amassing untold treasures, he eventually alienates everyone who matters, and loses his fortune.

Bitter and alone on his deathbed, the tycoon bleats the final word, "Rosebud!"

Despite longing for love and nurturing, Kane's life is so cluttered with objects that he misses the fact that *Rosebud,* his childhood sled—the symbol of innocence, of simpler times—the very object he so dearly misses, is stored in the cavernous basement beneath him. Into this space he's stuffed more treasures than could possibly be enjoyed in several lifetimes.

Mother Teresa cites loneliness, which is commonly noted in the United States, as the greatest form of poverty. As she addresses this pervasive form of impoverishment, she notes that so many American citizens are alone, uncared for, unwanted, unloved, and forgotten. The United States surgeon general, Vivek Murthy, also shares her take and attests that that our most prevalent health concern is not cancer, heart disease or obesity, but is isolation.[12] Amidst all the plenty and wealth this country has to offer, multitudes—hoarders in particular—starve of loneliness and isolation.

"Even if we act to erase material poverty," notes Robert Kennedy, in a 1968 speech he gave at University of Kansas, "there is another greater task, it is to confront the poverty of satisfaction—purpose and dignity—that afflicts us all….Too much and for too long, we seemed to have surrendered personal excellence and community values in the mere accumulation of material things."[13]

As a sidebar: What does it say about our culture that so many heterosexual men have no friends, and that women, overall, tend to live several years longer than they do?

Curiously, gay men, similar to the average female, seek out and thrive on the support of a large swath of individuals. Yet, loads of evidence points with concern to the many childhood bromances among hetero men that lapse into oblivion, which in turn, can adversely impact their health. Quite possibly, this is a topic for yet another book.

In the 1980's, study after study showed that social isolates were more likely to die during a given period than their more interactive neighbors. A more recent 2015 study at Brigham Young University, using data from 3.5 million people and spanned over 35 years, found that those who face loneliness, isolation, or even live alone see their risk of premature death rise 26 to 32 percent. Consider that in the United States, nearly a third of people older than 65 live alone; and by age 85, that number jumps to about half. Add this up, and it's easy to grasp why the surgeon general declares that loneliness is a serious public health epidemic.[14]

Loneliness has a tangible adverse impact on physical health in part because it enhances production of the stress hormone cortisol, which then suppresses immune function. Loneliness and isolation are linked to an increased risk of cardiovascular disease and stroke, as well as the progression of Alzheimer's.

With regard to mental health, it's no surprise that isolation is strongly associated with depression, suicide, anxiety, as well as fear and the perception of threat.

While consumerism serves as an attempt to fill the social void, far from curing it, the self-comparison and competition that arises as result, seems to have intensified to the extent that humans now seem to prey upon each other. Whereas social media—Facebook, Twitter, Pinterest, Linkedin and the like—try to bring people together, it also drives them apart.

Participation on Facebook or Instagram gives ample opportunity to quantify one's social standing. It's de rigeur to post photos of the delightful times enjoyed or to share sentiments: Hit *Like or Share this post if you have the best daughter or mom ever!* Or: *Please take note that I have thousands of friends and followers, while you only have a handful.*

Furthermore, unintentional boasts are common: *Look at me! See what a great, important life I'm living! Notice my excellent taste, how loved I am, how much I possess, how successful I am!* By pointing out abundance, what's lacking becomes all too evident.

Narcissism, bandied about a lot these days with reference to Donald Trump, is about extreme selfishness made manifest in those with a distorted, grandiose view of his or her talents and craves adulation. Narcissism in our culture also refers to self-absorption arising from the failure to distinguish the self from external objects.

Narcissism is not about vanity, but about the terror of nothingness. Our pervasive *Culture of Narcissism*, a term originally coined by author Christopher Lasch, exists in response to the void. It is fear of emptiness and a lack of meaning that's led to our cultural overload.

Plainly, something far more important than the issues that humans obsess and fret about are amiss. We humans, engaged in the all-consuming frenzy of environmental destruction and social dislocation, seek to squelch our unbearable pain. And comprehensive change, one far beyond our frenetic spending, is required to remedy it. Reappraisal of our entire view of life and of this world is requisite and the idea that one can or must go it alone is absurdly dangerous.

To change our worldview and, ultimately to improve our world for the better, humans must stand together. If not, everything falls apart.

ENDNOTES

Sources—The Who, What, Where and the When, but Not the Why or the How

---

INTRODUCTION: WHAT A DUMP!—TO HAVE AND TO HOLD EVER MORE

1. A. Pertusa et al., "Refining the Boundaries of Compulsive Hoarding," *Clinical Psychology Review,* 2010, Vol. 30: 371-386.

2. Randy Frost, "Causes of Hoarding," March 13, 2013, International OCD website: https://iocdf.org/, interview by Carly Bourne.

Chapter Two: Clutter Busters Strike Again—The Business of Clean Up

1. National Association of Professional Organizers website: http://www.napo.net/.

2. *The Fly Shop*, Marla Cilley's, Fly Lady website: http://shop.flylady.net/.

3. *Messies Anonymous* website: http://www.messies.com/.

Chapter Three: Animals do it, Humans do it—A Brief History of Hoarding

1. Randy Frost et al., "The Threat of the Housing Inspector: A Case of Hoarding," *Harvard Review*, ed. Richard Schwartz, 6 (1999): 270-278.

2. Randy Frost and Gail Steketee, *Stuff: Compulsive Hoarding and the Meaning of Things* (New York: Mariner Books, 2010).

3. Nicholas A Basbanes, *A Gentle Madness: Bibliophiles, Bibliomanes, and the Eternal Passion for Books* (New York: Henry Holt, 1999).

4. Basbanes.

5. Franz Lidz, *Ghosty Men: The Strange but True Story of the Collyer Brothers and My Uncle Arthur, New York's Greatest Hoarders* (New York: Bloomsbury, 2003).

Chapter Four: Collector, Packrat, or Hoarder?—It's a Fine Line

1. Randy Frost and Gail Steketee, *Stuff: Compulsive Hoarding and the Meaning of Things* (New York: Houghton Mifflin, 2010).

2. Dominick Bouckaert, "Collecting in Belgium," December 21, 2016, *Malt Maniacs* website: http://www.maltmaniacs.net/26 (2007).

3. Steven Winn, "Call them What You Will—Obsessive Compulsive Eccentrics, Materialist Philosophers or Pack-rat Artists—Collectors' 'Unruly Passions' Make Sense of Our World," *San Francisco Chronicle*, December 15, 2003.

4. Roger Butterfield, "Avery Brundage," *Life*, May 9, 2012: 201-202.

5. Werner Muensterberger, *Collecting: An Unruly Passion: Psychological Perspectives* (New Jersey: Princeton University Press, 1995).

6. Muensterberger.

CHAPTER FIVE: I'M COLLECTING AS FAST AS I CAN—OCD, AND OCD HOARDING AS A SUB-SET

1. Moshen Foroughipour et al., "Frequency of Obsessive-Compulsive Disorder in Patients with Multiple Sclerosis: A Cross-Sectional Study," *Journal of Research and Medical Science,* 3 (Mar; 17, 2012): 248–253.

2. Michael Drosnin, *Citizen Hughes: the Power, the Money and the Madness* (New York: Holt, Rinehart & Winston, 2004).

3. J. Samuels et al., "Hoarding in Obsessive Compulsive Disorder: Results from a Case-Control Study," *Behavior & Research Therapy,* Vol 40, Issue 5, 29 (March 2002): 517-528.

4. Kimberly Rae Miller, *Coming Clean* (New York: Houghton Mifflin Harcourt, 2013): 90.

5. Lorrin Koran, "The Pack Rat and the Neighborhood Trash House," speech given at the National Symposium of Professional Organizers, Millbrae, CA, March 16, 2000.

6. The National Institute of Mental Health, Obsessive Compulsive Disorders website: http://www.nimh.nih.gov/health/topics/obsessive-compulsive-disorder-ocd/index.shtml.

7. D. Greenberg et al., "Hoarding as a Psychiatric Symptom," *Journal of Clinical Psychiatry*, 51 (1990): 417-421.

8. Randy Frost and Gail Steketee, *Stuff: Compulsive Hoarding and the Meaning of Things* (New York: Mariner Books, 2010).

9. Jeffrey M. Welch et al., "Cortico-Striatal Synaptic Defects and OCD-Like Behaviours in Sapap3-Mutant Mice," *Nature*, 448, 894-900 (23 August 2007): 894-900.

10. R. O. Frost and R.C. Gross, "The Hoarding of Possessions," *Behavioral Research Therapy*, 31:4 (May 1993) 367-81.

11. Marco Grados, "Tourette's, OCD, ADHD: Closer Together than We Thought," *John Hopkins Psychiatry and Behavioral Sciences*, (Summer: 2009).

CHAPTER SIX: HOARDING CATS AND DOGS—LOVING ANIMALS TO DEATH

1. Kelly Luker, "Collective Concern," *Metro Santa Cruz*, December 26, 1996 to January 1, 1997.

2. Emily Carpenter, "Cats Found in Van in Ontario Hoarding Case," *The Argus Observer*, November 13, 2014.

3. Karen Cassiday, "What is Animal Hoarding?" February 2017, Crime Clean-AZ website: http://crimeclean-az.com/what-is-animal-hoarding/.

4. The Hoarding of Animals Research Consortium, July 2013, website: http://vet.tufts.edu/hoarding/index.html.

5. Martha Willman, "Cat Count Climbs to Nearly 600 as Animal Rescuer is Arrested," *Los Angeles Times*: July 9, 1997.

6. "Animal Hoarding Case Study: Vikki Kittles; Winning the Case Against Cruelty," *Animal Legal Defense Fund,* August 2014, website: http://aldf.org/resources/laws-cases/animal-hoarding-case-study-vikki-kittles/.

7. Kelly Luker, "American Gothic: How Family Feuds and Mismanagement Reduced a Once Famous Vacation Playland to Scattered Shards of Real Estate," *MetroActive Santa Cruz News*, May 21-27, 1998.

8. Shawn Skager, "Film to Focus on Aftermath of Enumclaw Incident," *Enumclaw Courier Herald*, April, 2009.

CHAPTER SEVEN: EVOLUTION GONE GONZO—CONTRIBUTING FACTORS AND HOARDING RESEARCH

1. Werner Muensterberger, *Collecting: An Unruly Passion: Psychological Perspectives* (New Jersey: Princeton University Press, 1995).

2. Randy Frost and Lee Shuer, "Compulsive Hoarding," *Scientific American*, February 26, 2013.

3. Jack F. Samuels et al, "Prevalence and Correlates of Hoarding Behavior in a Community-Based Sample," *Behavior Research Therapy*, 46:7 (July 2008): 836-844.

4. R. Frost and R.C. Gross, "The Hoarding of Possessions," *Behavior Research Therapy*, 31: (1993): 367-381.

5. Wheaton M. et al, "Characterizing the Hoarding Phenotype in Individuals with OCD: Associations with Comorbidity, Severity and Gender," *Journal of Anxiety Disorders*, 22 (2008): 243–152.

6. Frost, 367-381.

7. Jane Collingswood, "The Genetics of Compulsive Hoarding," *Animal Hoarding News*, September 27, 2009, website: http://animalhoardinginfo.blogspot.com/.

8. R. Frost and R.C. Gross, "The Hoarding of Possessions," *Behavior Research Therapy*, 31 (1993): 367-381.

9. "The Infinite Mind: Hoarding and Clutter." A radio interview with Dr. Sanjay Saxena, Director of the Obsessive-Compulsive Disorder Research Program at the University of California at Los Angeles, July 31, 2002 (originally aired August 12, 2002).

10. Collingswood..

11. D.D. Christensen and J. H. Greist, "The Challenge of Obsessive-Compulsive Disorder Hoarding," *Primary Psychiatry*, 8 (2001): 79-86.

12. Sanjay Saxena, "Neurobiology and Treatment of Compulsive Hoarding," *Cambridge Journals:* CNS Spectr Supplement 14, 13:9 (September 2008): 29-36.

13. Maia Szalavitz, "Inside the Hoarder's Brain: A Unique Problem With Decision-Making," *Time*, August 7, 2012.

14. Szalavitz.

15. Szalavitz.

16. J.M. Schwarts et al., "Systemic Changes in Cerebral Glucose Metabolic Rate After Successful Behavior Modification Treatment of Obsessive-Compulsive Disorder," *Arch Gen Psychiatry,* 53 (1996): 109-113.

17. Judith Rapoport, *The Boy Who Couldn't Stop Washing* (New York, New American Library, 1989) 8-9.

18. Rapoport, 94.

19. Rapoport, 8-9.

20. S.W. Anderson et al., "A Neural Basis for Collecting Behaviour in Humans," *Brain,* 128 (2005): 201–212.

21. E. Dykens and B. Shah, "Psychiatric Disorders in Prader-Willi Syndrome," *CNS Drugs,* 17 (2003): 167-178.

22. D. Gothelf et al., "Obsessive-Compulsive Disorder in Patients with Velocardiofacial Syndrome," *American Journal of Medical Genetics,* Part B, Neuropsychiatric Genetics 126 (2004): 99–105.

23. J.F. Samuels et al., "Hoarding in Obsessive-Compulsive Disorder: Results from the OCD Collaborative Genetics Study," *Behaviour Research and Therapy,* 43 (2007): 673–686.

24. Rapoport, 14.

25. J.P. Hwang et al., "Hoarding Behavior in Dementia: A Preliminary Report," *American Journal of Geriatric Psychiatry,* 6:4 (Fall, 1998): 285-289.

26. D. Greenberg et al., "Hoarding as a Psychiatric Symptom," *Journal of Clinical Psychiatry,* 51 (1990): 417–421.

27. Mental Health Association website: http://mentalhealthsd.org/programs/ich/pcori.

CHAPTER EIGHT: LOOK, MA, NO MORE STUFF!—THERAPEUTIC TREATMENTS FOR HOARDERS

1. Jack Schwartz and Beverly Beyette, *Brain Lock: Free Yourself from Obsessive-Compulsive Behavior* (New York: Regan Books, 1996).

2. Schwartz, 53.

3. Schwartz, 53.

4. Kathleen DesMaisons, *Potatoes Not Prozac: Simple Solutions for Sugar Sensitivity* (New York: Simon & Schuster 2008).

5. Sanjay Saxena, et al., "Paroxetine Treatment of Compulsive Hoarding," *Journal of Psychiatric Research*, (June 21, 2006).

6. DesMaisons.

7. John Ratey and Catherine Johnson, *Shadow Syndromes: The Mild Forms of Major Mental Disorders that Sabotage Us* (New York: Bantam Books, 1998) 333-334.

8. Sanjay Saxena, "Neurobiology and Treatment of Compulsive Hoarding," *Cambridge Journals:* CNS Spectr Supplement 14, 13:9 (September 2008) 29-36.

9. Katherine Q. Seelye, "Kitty Dukakis, a Beneficiary of Electroshock Therapy, Emerges as Its Evangelist," *The New York Times:* A13 (January 1, 2017).

10. Ian Osborne, *Tormenting Thoughts and Secret Rituals: The Hidden Epidemic of Obsessive-Compulsive Disorder* (New York: Dell, 1998) 108.

11. Saxena, 29-36.

12. Jeffrey Schwartz and Beverly Beyette, *Brain Lock: Free Yourself from Obsessive-Compulsive Behavior* (New York: Regan Books, 1996) 53.

13. Anne Jacobson, "Cognitive Behavioral Therapy Can Cut Compulsive Hoarding," *Clinical Psychiatry News:* 29:6 (June 2001).

14. Randy Frost, "Hoarding," *20/20,* ABCNews.com, October 22 1999, moderated interview.

15. Schwartz.

16. Edmund Bourne, *The Anxiety & Phobia Workbook,* 6th edition (Oakland: New Harbinger Publications, 2015).

17. Frost.

18. Denise Linn, *Feng Shui for the Soul,* (Carlsbad: Hay House, 2000).

19. Marie Kondo, *The Life Changing Magic of Tidying Up: the Japanese Art of Organizing and Decluttering* (Berkeley, CA: Ten-Speed Press, 2014).

20. Flannery Dean,"The Dark Side of Kondo Living: The Japanese Tidying Guru is Part of Our Culture's Trip Down a Dysfunctional Road," *Maclean's,* (February 20, 2016).

21. Marilyn Luber, Ed, *Eye Movement Desensitization and Reprocessing (EMDR)Therapy Scripted Protocols and Summary Sheets: Treating Anxiety, Obsessive-Compulsive, and Mood-Related Conditions,* 1st Edition (New York: Springer Publishing, 2016).

CHAPTER NINE: LIGHT AT DUMPSTER'S BOTTOM—COMMUNITIES AND NEIGHBORS INTERFACE WITH HOARDERS

1. Marina Malikoff, "Hoarding," *Santa Cruz Sentinel* (October 3, 1999).

2. Jim Walker, "It Takes a Village: Neighbors Must Unite To Fight Public Nuisances," *Los Angeles Times* (October 10, 1999).

3. Sabin Russell, "Obsessive Hoarding Can be Mental Illness," *San Francisco Chronicle* (December 26, 1997).

4. Kimberly Rae Miller, *Coming Clean* (New York: Houghton Mifflin Harcourt, 2013).

CHAPTER TEN: TILL TRASH DO US PART—LIVING WITH OR WITHOUT YOUR BELOVED HOARDER

1. Carolyn Tyler, "Woman Found Mummified in San Francisco Home May have Died Years Ago," *Eyewitness News*, ABC, April, 7, 2015.

2. Avi Salzman, "Court Ruling Clears Mother in Son's Suicide," *The New York Times* (Aug 29, 2006).

3. Fugen Nezieroglu and Katherine Donnelly, *Children of Hoarders: How to Minimize Conflict, Reduce the Clutter, and Improve Your Relationship* (Oakland: New Harbinger Publications, 2013).

CHAPTER ELEVEN: SCRAPING OUT THE DEAD—HOARDERS WHO DIE AMIDST THEIR STUFF

1. N.R. Kleinfield, "The Lonely Death of George Bell," *The New York Times*, October 17, 2015.

2. Charlotte Alter, "Hoarder Dies When House Collapses From All Her Stuff," *Cheshire Citizen*, June 16, 2014.

3. Hannah Buchdahl, "What Happens When a Hoarder Dies?" *Newsweek*, January 26, 2011.

4. Buchdahl.

5. George Brown, "Mummified Remains Found in Dead Hoarder's Home," *The Washington Post*, March 8, 2011.

6. Kathryn Vercillo, "10 Horrifying Stories of Hoarders Who Died in their Stuff," *Top Tenz, People*, October 23, 2014.

7. Kleinfeld, 201.

CHAPTER TWELVE: GOT AFFLUENZA?—THE SPIRITUAL RAMIFICATIONS OF OUR JUNK

1. John de Graff et al., *Affluenza: How Overconsumption is Killing Us and How to Fight Back* (San Francisco: Brette Kohler Publishers, 3rd Edition, 2014).

2. *Reverend Billy and the Church of Stop Shopping*: Wikipedia; last modified, April 11, 2015.

3. Peter Mitchell and John Scheffel, Ed, *Understanding Power: the Indispensable Chomsky* (New York: New Press, 2002), 183-182.

4. Harold Kushner, *When All You've Ever Wanted Isn't Enough* (New York: Summit Books, 1986.)

5. Jane Hammerslough, *Dematerializing: Taming the Power of Possessions* (New York: Perseus, 2001) 161.

6. Joshua Fields Milburn and Ryan Nicodemus, *Minimalism: Live a Meaningful Life* (Missoula: Asymmetrical Press, 2016).

7. Alex Williams, "Why Self-Help Guru James Altucher Only Owns 15 Things," *The New York Times*, August, 6, 2016.

8. Williams.

9. Williams.

10. Williams.

11. Williams.

12. Simon Rogers, "Bobby Kennedy on GDP: 'Measures Everything Except that Which is Worthwhile,'" *The Guardian*, May 24, 2012. (Excerpted from Robert Kennedy's speech at University of Kansas, March 18, 1968.).

13. Billy Baker, "The Biggest Threat Facing Middle-Age Men Isn't Smoking or Obesity. It's Loneliness," *The Boston Globe*, March 9, 2017.

14. Baker.

ABOUT THE AUTHORS

WILLIAM STRUBBE IS AN AUTHOR, playwright, journalist, photographer and painter living on an Israeli kibbutz. While he still periodically declutters friends' and clients' homes, his forthcoming novel *The Diary of Annelies Marie Levenson: If Anne Frank had Lived*, revolves on the premise that Anne Frank survived WWII, and on her 30th birthday begins writing her diaries anew.

Janice Strubbe Wittenberg's previous works include her award-winning novel, *The Worship of Walker Judson* and *The Rebellious Body: Reclaim Your Life from Environmental Illness or Chronic Fatigue Syndrome*. Formerly, a crisis outreach specialist for Santa Cruz County Mental Health, she resides in Aptos, California with her husband, John, their two cats and her beloved covey of chickens. The flock provides inspiration for her forthcoming novel, *The Fluster Clucker,* about a rooster who aspires to be human.

Please visit Janice's Website:
Strubbe-Wittenberg.com
Honest book reviews are apreciated.

www.ingramcontent.com/pod-product-compliance
Lightning Source LLC
Chambersburg PA
CBHW051648040426
42446CB00009B/1042